LEGALITY
OF
STUDENT DISCIPLINARY
PRACTICES

by

EDWARD C. BOLMEIER

Professor Emeritus of Education
Duke University

THE MICHIE COMPANY

Law Publishers

CHARLOTTESVILLE, VIRGINIA

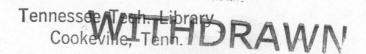

CONTENTS

FOREWORD

Before deciding on a research project on school law for publication, the author consulted colleagues, school officials, school teachers and legal authorities as to what they considered the most pertinent and perplexing problems confronting the public schools today. They were virtually unanimous in specifying *student discipline* as the problem with which they were most concerned. Articles in school journals and law reviews share the opinion.

Disobedience, lawlessness and violence in the public schools are increasing at an alarming rate. Undoubtedly this trend is merely a manifestation of what is taking place throughout our society. The breakdown of family solidarity and parental authority, and the failure of governmental control over crime certainly contribute to the deterioration of discipline in the public schools. This, however, does not obviate the responsibility of school officials to deal directly with the problem. After all, the primary purpose of the school is to develop good citizenship.

The general practice of school officials to improve student discipline is to formulate rules and regulations to prevent disobedience and disruption in order to carry out the educational processes. When such rules and regulations are violated, school authorities often exercise their prerogatives by resorting to some form of punitive action designed to improve behavior.

Frequently the rules and regulations, and particularly the manner in which they are enforced, cause parents and students to challenge the propriety and legality of the school officials' action.

Admittedly this publication does not offer solutions to the vexing problems of student discipline. If it could, it would be a "best seller." The main purpose of the book is to draw attention to court cases which determine the legal principles to serve as guidelines for adopting practices most conducive to better student discipline.

E. C. B.

Durham, N.C.
May, 1976

Chapter 1

INTRODUCTION

§ 1.1. Blame and responsibility for student misconduct.

Confronted with escalating misconduct, disobedience, disruption and violence of students in the public schools, school officials and others are perplexed in determining the causes and in finding effective and legal disciplinary procedures to cope with such wrong-doings.

The school. In some instances the schools themselves are unduly blamed for student misconduct. But as bad as misbehavior and viciousness are in some school systems, there is no evidence that such conditions in the schools are worse than, or even as bad as, in other areas of society. It has been stated that "schools are nothing but extensions of the streets." The violence, lawlessness and vandalism which prevail in some of our public schools throughout the nation are merely faint reflections of what takes place daily in our general society on the part of adults as well as youths.

The legislature. Legislatures, too, are frequently accused of being at fault for failing to enact legislation which would authorize and compel school officials to apply effective disciplinary procedures to alleviate student misbehavior. Most states *do have* statutory provisions pertaining to permissible or required methods of disciplining unruly students. Significantly, however, such provisions must be within constitutional limits.

The judiciary. In recent years the courts have been the main target of blame for the laxity of student discipline, by restricting school officials in the enforcement of their rules and regulations concerning conduct. Judges have occasionally been described as being "soft hearted and soft headed" in their obligatory judicial acts of upholding students' rights. Even though it would be administratively expedient to permit school authorities to exercise their discretion in resorting to impulsive punitive action for violation of school board rules and regulations, the constitutional rights of all individuals — including students — must be protected. As one writer suggests:

> Recent so-called liberal court decisions are going to have, ultimately, a good effect upon the operation of our schools. It can't help but be a wonderful thing to know that your child or mine will be treated as a thinking, sensitive person whose rights will not be abrogated by the impulsive whim of a momentarily angry school administrator. (Donald E. Smith, "Surviving Student Behavior Problems," *American Secondary Education,* p. 29, June 1975)

As a matter of fact the problem of dealing with unruly students necessitates cooperative effort on the part of many — especially school personnel. This is expressed in an article which states:

While it may be partially correct to place some of the blame on an apathetic society or lax insecure parents, much of the responsibility must be shared by poorly trained, bored teachers and the complacent administrators as well.

The burden of the restoration of authority within the schools does not rest upon teachers and administrators alone. Parents, the community and all others who come in contact with the student, shape his thinking and must share in the partnership. However, our educational system which has effectively shaped social policy in the past must again rally to bring order and security to our youth. (Hal W. Seaton and Regis Q. McKnight, "Lack of Authority: A Crisis in Education," *American Secondary Education,* pp. 6-7, March 1975)

Congressional cooperation. Concern and responsibility for dealing with student violence is evidenced by the Report of the Subcommittee to investigate Juvenile Delinquency, *Our Nation's Schools — A Report Card: "A" in School Violence and Vandalism* (U. S. Government Printing Office, Washington, D.C. (1975)).

Under the chairmanship of Senator Birch Bayh, the report was released "to direct the attention of the Congress and the American people to a most disturbing and costly problem — violence and vandalism in the schools of our nation" (*Id.* at 1).

After several hearings with schoolmen and others concerned with the problem, Senator Bayh introduced the "Juvenile Delinquency in the Schools Act of 1975," and recently added an extensive amendment thereto, on June 17, 1975.

Senator Bayh made it clear in his opening statement at the hearings that the problem was one requiring cooperative effort. Brief excerpts from his statement follow:

> I must emphasize, however, that I do not believe those of us in Washington can, or should, make these educational decisions and policies which are quite properly made by people most familiar with the realities and peculiarities of specific, individual situations.... Rather, I intend to develop legislation which can provide a vehicle through which our local, state and federal governments, along with our private sector, can pool their experiences and resources to help students, teachers, parents and administrators secure the type of atmosphere in our schools in which education can best take place.
> ... We also intend to explore the area of student, teacher and parent rights and responsibilities as well as how legitimate and necessary school rules can best be improved and enforced to insure firm, but even-handed discipline in our schools (*Id.* at 2).

§ 1.2. Nature and scope of disciplinary practices.

The term "discipline" generally refers to action taken by the school authorities against a student because his conduct, as distinct from his academic performance, falls short of conforming to certain school standards.

Ever since the beginning of American education it has been customary for school officials to formulate rules and regulations designed to maintain discipline. Failure to conform to the rules and regulations subjects the students to punitive action as a means for enforcement.

The earliest form of punitive action was "corporal punishment," an infliction of physical pain designed to defer future misconduct. It was based on the old Latin concept, *in loco parentis,* meaning that the teacher was authorized to act in place of the parent for the maintenance of proper conduct. Although the original meaning and purpose of the *in loco parentis* doctrine have long since passed, the term is still used as a defense in parental versus school authority in issues beyond that of just corporal punishment.

With the gradual diminution of corporal punishment as a deterrent to misbehavior, the schools have resorted more recently to exclusionary actions such as suspension and expulsion. Such actions are frequently contested in the courts, and since they involve constitutional questions, the federal courts are called upon for interpretations and rulings.

The scope of disciplinary practices considered in this investigation goes beyond that of *corporal punishment, suspension,* and *expulsion.* It also includes punishment by *deprivation of school privileges* for failure to conform to school board rules and regulations.

§ 1.3. Organization of issues discussed in this publication.

Chapter 2. The In Loco Parentis Doctrine. A discussion of this doctrine would not necessarily be included in this publication were it not for the fact that its original purpose has been expanded to cover litigious controls other than corporal punishment. Many court cases indicate that it is becoming an obsolete doctrine and will likely be discarded as a defense for disciplinary action.

Chapter 3. Due Process and School Discipline. This issue is of comparatively recent origin as a legal consideration in student disciplinary practices. The term is frequently mentioned in writings without really defining its meaning. Even the judiciary refers to "due process" as "an elusive concept." *Procedural* due process came into sharp focus as a litigious issue with the decision rendered in the *Gault* case, whereby juveniles are entitled to the same constitutional rights accorded adults.

Chapter 4. Administration of Corporal Punishment. Corporal punishment was the first punitive measure used for the purpose of disciplining students. A review of court cases indicates it is rather ineffective as a deterrent for misconduct — especially at the secondary school level. This is understandable in view of the fact that the superior size and strength of some high school students would jeopardize the physical welfare of a teacher who would attempt to inflict such punishment.

Chapter 5. Exclusionary Practices: Suspension — Expulsion. The original intent in organizing this publication was to treat suspension and expulsion in separate chapters. However, after reviewing many court cases involving exclusionary practices it was noted that the terms are used interchangeably — even in the reporting of a single court case. It is difficult to differentiate between "short term" and "long term" suspensions. The recent decision of the United States Supreme Court (*Goss v. Lopez*) in stipulating how long a suspension can last without applying formal due process procedures, has not resulted in conclusive clarification.

Chapter 6. Unorthodox Practices of Disciplining. This chapter has been planned for making reference to litigated issues concerning student discipline other than the more familiar practices of corporal punishment, suspension and expulsion. Most of the cases referred to in this chapter have to do with deprivation of school privileges for students who fail to conform to local rules and regulations of questionable merit.

§ 1.4. Selection and treatment of court cases.

The cases referred to in this publication merely represent a sampling of all those dealing with disciplinary practices. Only a few of the early cases have been selected for historical purposes. The great majority of cases represent those that have been found in the latest case reporters. An attempt has been made to select approximately the same number for each side of a litigated issue. The author is well aware that, in all probability, more pertinent court decisions will be rendered on controversial student disciplinary practices before this manuscript has gone through the necessary publication processes.

Chapter 2
THE IN LOCO PARENTIS DOCTRINE

§ 2.1. Origin of the doctrine.

Ever since the beginning of education in America, and particularly during the private-school era, the teacher possessed limited discretionary authority in governing pupils. The authority derives from the common-law doctrine referred to as *in loco parentis,* which, when translated, means "in place of the parent." The classic phrase may be traced to *Blackstone's Commentaries:*

> A parent may also delegate part of his parental authority, during his life, to the tutor or schoolmaster of his child; who is then *in loco parentis,* and has such a portion of the power of the parent, viz. that the restraint and correction, as may be necessary to answer the purposes for which he is employed. (*Blackstone, Commentaries of the Laws of England,* p. 453 (T. Cooley ed. 1884))

It is significant to note that the last words of the Blackstonian phrase *(as may be necessary to answer the purpose for which he is employed)* do not imply that the doctrine authorizes school authorities to *completely* displace parental authority during the school day. Disregard for this limitation is cause for much of the litigation referred to in following sections of this chapter.

§ 2.2. Limited scope of the doctrine.

Usually the *in loco parentis* principle is applied only in cases of pupil discipline. However, this legal principle *is not absolute.* For example, a statutory provision in the Illinois laws broadens the scope of the teacher's authority and responsibility beyond that of maintaining discipline. In an applicable case (*Woodman v. Litchfield Community School Dist. No. 12,* 242 N.E.2d 780 (Ill. App. 1968)) the Appellate Court of Illinois, Fifth District, takes cognizance of the statute in quoting the following statement:

> Teachers . . . shall maintain discipline in the schools. In all matters relating to the discipline in and conduct of the schools and the school children, they stand in the relation of parents and guardians to the pupils. This relationship shall extend to all activities connected with the school program and may be exercised at any time for the safety and supervision of the pupils in the absence of their parents or guardians (*Id.* at 782).

The Court's rationale in its decision is expressed in the following statement:

> This statutory enactment would protect a teacher from liability for mere negligence in supervision or maintaining discipline because

of the status conferred; that of a parent or guardian in relation to all the pupils in the classroom. No liability would attach to a parent or one having the relation of parent absent an event constituting willful or wanton conduct (*Id.* at 782).

The more prevalent line of reasoning with respect to the scope of the *in loco parentis* theory is indicated in a decision of a teacher liability case (*Morris v. Ortiz,* 103 Ariz. 119, 437 P.2d 652 (1968)), where a dissenting judge on the Supreme Court of Arizona stated:

The relationship of a public school teacher to his pupil is in some respects in loco parentis. Having the right to control and supervise the pupil, there is a correlative duty to act as a reasonable and prudent parent would in like circumstances. . . . The rationale of in loco parentis does not however apply in determining liability for a negligent tort against the pupil. In most jurisdictions the parent is not liable for negligent tort against his child, but the public school teacher may be (*Id.* at 657).

. . . No one can deny that few sectors of public and private existence are safe from risks to life and limb; the schoolyard, the classroom, the shop class, the chemistry laboratory certainly have their dangers and their risks. Teachers presumptively endowed with superior skill, judgment, intelligence and foresight, must fulfill the strong duties arising from their public position by exercising care commensurate with the immaturity of their charges and the importance of their trust (*Id.* at 658).

So the *in loco parentis* theory has been expanded so far in recent decades that the schools have assumed authority to enact regulations designed to protect the morals, welfare and safety of pupils and to determine their school attendance, appearance and curricular activities with or without parental concurrence. Consequently numerous court cases have arisen on the issue of parental versus school authority over the pupil with respect to many matters other than the discipline of the pupil, for which the *in loco parentis* doctrine was originally conceived.

§ 2.3. Treatment of injury or sickness.

The limited authority of a teacher over the pupil in matters "necessary to answer the purposes for which he is employed" is exemplified in an early Pennsylvania case (*Guerrieri v. Tyson,* 147 Pa. Super. 239, 24 A.2d 468 (1942)) where a teacher attempted to treat a student's infected finger by immersing it in scalding water against his will, which aggravated the infection and permanently disfigured his hand.

The Court agreed to the delegated parental authority implied from the relationship of teacher and pupils, but in ruling against the teacher in the instant case, the Court stated:

> ...a teacher may inflict reasonable corporal punishment on a pupil to enforce discipline ... but there is no implied delegation of authority to exercise her lay judgment, as

a parent may, in the matter of the treatment of injury or disease suffered by a pupil.... (*Id.* at 469).

A case (*Duda v. Gaines*, 12 N.J. Super. 326, 79 A.2d 695 (1951)) refers to alleged negligence of a teacher, standing *in loco parentis*, who failed to obtain medical assistance for a school pupil who was injured during football practice. The action was taken by the infant's guardian *ad litem*.

In rendering judgment for the defendant teacher, the Court ruled there was insufficient proof to indicate the existence of the alleged emergency, and accordingly made the following statement:

> The emergency from which would arise the stipulated legal duty can be said to exist when a reasonable man having the knowledge of facts known to the teachers or which they might reasonably be expected to know would recognize a pressing necessity for medical aid, and the dictates of humanity, duty and fair dealing would require that there be put in the boy's reach such medical care and other assistance as the situation might in reason demand so that the pupil might be relieved of his hurt and more serious consequences be avoided (*Id.* at 696).

In order to avoid liability of teachers for rendering first-aid assistance to injured or ill pupils in emergencies, Marlin M. Volz, former dean of the Louisville Law School, makes the following recommendations:

Teachers should be cautioned: (1) to treat or

medicate to a pupil without the parent's consent only in an emergency; (2) not to substitute their judgment for that of parents in deciding whether a condition should be treated which is not of an emergency nature; (3) not to render more first aid or treatment than is necessary to protect the child until the parents can be contacted or expert medical care obtained; (4) to use conservative and conventional first-aid methods and not to experiment or utilize untried procedures; (5) to report incidents promptly to the principal's office so that the parents or medical personnel may be contacted, where indicated; (6) not to medicate or treat beyond their training or skill — a nurse or person with medical training or experience may go further than an untrained person but even such person should limit treatment to emergency first aid without a parent's consent; (7) not to send a seriously injured or ill pupil home without proper escort or without first ascertaining that a parent is home (*Law and the School Principal,* ch. 6, p. 127, The W. H. Anderson Co. (1961)).

§ 2.4. Compulsory school attendance.

Innumerable court cases have evolved from the doctrine of *in loco parentis* which were never intended in the earliest application. For example, in an early case (*State v. Bailey,* 157 Ind. 324, 61 N.E. 730 (1901)) the issue of parental versus state authority over the control of the pupil developed when a parent was charged with having neglected and refused to send his child to school, thereby violating the provisions of the state's

compulsory school attendance law. The parent alleged
that the law was unconstitutional because "it invades
the natural right of a man to govern and control his own
children." In refuting the claims of the parent, and
rendering a decision against him, the Court stated:

> One of the most important natural duties of
> the parent is his obligation to educate his child,
> and this duty he owes not to the child only, but
> to the commonwealth. If he neglects to
> perform it or willfully refuses to do so, he may
> be coerced by law to execute such civil
> obligation. The welfare of the child and the
> best interests of society require that the state
> shall exert its sovereign authority to secure to
> the child the opportunity to acquire an
> education (*Id.* at 732).

The courts have disagreed as to whether the schools,
rather than the parent, may determine the type of a
school a pupil must attend. The landmark Oregon case
(*Pierce v. Society of Sisters of Holy Names, Etc.,* 268
U.S. 510, 45 S. Ct. 571 (1925)) demonstrates the
nonapplicability of *in loco parentis,* where the
constitutional protection of parents' right to send their
children to schools of their own choice is concerned. The
following classic declaration of the U. S. Supreme Court
has been quoted often and generally unchallenged:

> ... we think it entirely plain that the Act of
> 1922 unreasonably interferes with the liberty
> of parents and guardians to direct the
> upbringing and education of children under
> their control .... The fundamental theory of
> liberty upon which all governments in this

Union repose excludes any general power of the state to standardize its children by forcing them to accept instruction from public teachers only. The child is not the mere creature of the state; those who nurture him and direct his destiny have the right, coupled with the high duty, to recognize and prepare him for additional obligations (*Id.* at 573).

Some parents who have been dissatisfied with the public school educational opportunities available have sought to satisfy compulsory school attendance requirements by providing *home instruction* rather than by sending their children to either public or nonpublic schools. The legality of the practice cannot be determined simply or conclusively because of the variations in statutory provision and the interpretation placed upon them by the courts. Nevertheless, *under certain conditions,* home instruction has been, and still is, sanctioned as satisfying compulsory school attendance requirements.

The judiciary is likely to condone the home instruction — providing it is equivalent to that afforded by the public school. A case in point (*State v. Massa,* 95 N.J. Super. 382, 231 A.2d 252 (1967)) is where a mother convinced the court that the home instruction she provided for her daughter was effective in attaining academic results and at least equivalent to that which could have been attained in a public or private school of her district.

School authorities who attempted to force attendance at a public school claimed that the home instruction, in lieu of public school instruction, lacked the social experiences such as might be provided by association with a number of classmates. The court, however, was not convinced by that argument and took the stand that "all children shall be educated, not that they shall be educated in a particular way."

But according to some jurisdictions home instruction cannot satisfy the compulsory school attendance requirements because it *cannot* be "equivalent" to that of public school instruction in *social* development of the child. In an applicable case (*Stephens v. Bongart,* 15 N.J. Misc. 80, 189 A. 131 (1937)) the parents of the two boys, ages eleven and twelve, withdrew their children from public school and instituted a program of home instruction. School authorities then charged the parents with a violation of the state's compulsory school attendance law and brought them before the court.

Among the deficiencies found in the home instruction program was that it lacked the ability to develop attitudes and to create a social setting in which children might be trained to deal with their playmates and friends as a part of a social group. After pointing to the great value derived from the social contact, Judge Seigler declared:

> I incline to the opinion that education is no longer concerned merely with the acquisition of facts; the instilling of worthy habits, attitudes, appreciations, and skills is far more important than mere imparting of subject-matter. A primary objective of education to-day is the development of character and good citizenship. Education

must impart to the child the way to live. This brings me to the belief that, in a cosmopolitan area such as we live in, with all the complexities of life, and our reliance upon others to carry out the functions of education, it is almost impossible for a child to be adequately taught in his home. I cannot conceive how a child can receive in the home instruction and experiences in group activity and in social outlook in any manner or form comparable to that provided in the public school (*Id.* at 137).

§ 2.5. Control over vaccinations.

The issue of vaccinations as a condition for public school attendance has been litigated frequently. Early laws requiring compulsory school attendance, as well as vaccinations of pupils, raised conflicts of opinion as to whether a parent was guilty of violating the compulsory school attendance law if his child was sent to school but denied admission therein by reason of not having complied with the vaccination requirement. This constituted another question regarding the validity of the *in loco parentis* doctrine.

At first the courts applied a strict construction to the compulsory school law, holding that parents must send their children to school, but having done that, regardless of the fact that the children were denied admission for failure to comply with the valid vaccination regulations, the parent had fulfilled the requirement of the compulsory school attendance law and could not be convicted for violation of the vaccination requirement. That judicial reasoning, however, was soon discarded.

Beginning with a New York case (*People v. Ekerold,* 211 N.Y. 386, 105 N.E. 670 (1914)) the early trend was reversed, and since that time the courts have generally held that parents are guilty of violating the compulsory school attendance laws even when the children are sent to school but denied admission because of failure to meet vaccination requirements. In *People v. Ekerold,* the court based its decision on legislative intent rather than on strict construction of the statute. The court pointed out that it was readily apparent that the legislature, in passing another law requiring vaccination as a condition for admission, did not intend that one should be used as an excuse to disobey the other.

In commenting on its decision the court stated:

> It does not require much spirit of prophecy to foresee what will follow a contrary construction of the statutes. If a parent may escape all obligation under the statute requiring him to send his children to school by simply alleging that he does not believe in vaccination, the policy of the state to give some education to all children, if necessary by compelling measures, will become more or less of a farce under existing legislation (*Id.* at 672).

The majority of cases evolving from violation of the compulsory school attendance laws where vaccination is a mandated condition for attendance are based upon religious beliefs. A case in point (*Anderson v. State,* 84

Ga. App. 259, 65 S.E.2d 848 (1951)) arose in Georgia in 1951.

Facts of that case indicated that: (1) the county nurse attempted to vaccinate the children against certain contagious diseases; (2) the defendant parents objected to the vaccination of the children on the ground that it was in conflict with their religious beliefs; (3) the parents believed in divine healing through faith rather than taking vaccination or immunization against disease; (4) the children returned to school but were denied admission for noncompliance with the vaccination requirement; and (5) the court then held the parents guilty of violating the compulsory school attendance law of the state. In commenting on the pertinent facts of the case the court concluded:

> Liberty of conscience is one thing. License to endanger the lives of others by practices contrary to statutes passed for the public safety and in reliance upon modern medical knowledge is another.... The defendants in this case sought to comply with their duty to send their children to school but at the same time usurp the prerogative of the school authorities, and also undertook to fix the rules under which they should attend. Their contention therefore that they did actually enroll the children unvaccinated constitutes no valid defense.... Such a contention is unsound for the reason that an offer to do a thing only upon waiver of the conditions precedent thereto amounts to no offer at all (*Id.* at 852).

Another case (*Cude v. State,* 237 Ark. 927, 377 S.W.2d

816 (1964)) involving religious objections to the
vaccination requirement is cited. In this case parents
not only refused to have their children vaccinated, but
refused to accept them back into the home if they should
be vaccinated.

The court was unanimous in agreeing that refusal to
comply with the compulsory school attendance law was
in violation of a constitutional provision which was
interpreted as meaning that "anyone has the right to
worship God in the manner of his own choice, but it does
not mean that he can engage in religious practices
inconsistent with the peace, safety and health of the
inhabitants of the State, and it does not mean that
parents, on religious grounds, have the right to deny
their children an education" (*Id.* at 818-19).

The force of compulsory public school attendance, as
well as *in loco parentis,* was greatly reduced with the
much publicized landmark decision in the case (*Wisconsin v. Yoder,* 406 U.S. 205 (1972)) where the High
Court upheld Amish parents who had refused to send
their children to school beyond the eighth grade.

The case report indicates that the parents ". . .
believed, in accordance with the tenets of Old Order
Amish communities generally, that their children's
attendance at high school, public or private, was
contrary to the Amish religion and way of life. They
believed that by sending their children to high school,
they would not only expose themselves to the danger
of the censure of the church community, but, as found
by the county court, also endanger their own salvation
and that of their children" (*Id.* at 209).

Moreover, they contended that:

> Formal high school education beyond the eighth grade is contrary to Amish beliefs, not only because it places Amish children in an environment hostile to Amish beliefs with increasing emphasis on competition in class work and sports and with pressure to conform to the styles, manners, and ways of the peer group, but also because it takes them away from their community, physically and emotionally, during the crucial and formative adolescent period of life. During this period, the children must acquire Amish attitudes favoring manual work and self-reliance and the specific skills needed to perform the adult role of an Amish farmer or housewife. They must learn to enjoy physical labor (*Id.* at 211).

That the state (school) could not take the place of the parent in determining where the child should be educated is indicated in the following judicial passages:

> Thus, a State's interest in universal education, however highly we rank it, is not totally free from a balancing process when it impinges on fundamental rights and interests, such as those specifically protected by the Free Exercise Clause of the First Amendment, and the traditional interest of parents with respect to the religious unbringing of their children so long as they, in the words of *Pierce*, "prepare [them] for additional obligations" (*Id.* at 214).
>
> The essence of all that has been said and written on the subject is that only those interests of the highest order and those not otherwise served can overbalance legitimate

claims to the free exercise of religion. We can accept it as settled, therefore, that, however strong the State's interest in universal compulsory education, it is by no means absolute to the exclusion or subordination of all other interests (*Id.* at 215).

The history and culture of Western civilization reflect a strong tradition of parental concern for the nurture and upbringing of their children. This primary role of the parents in the upbringing of their children is now established beyond debate as an enduring American tradition. (*Id.* at 232).

In the face of our consistent emphasis on the central values underlying the Religion Clauses in our constitutional scheme of government, we cannot accept a *parens patriae* claim of such all-encompassing scope and with such sweeping potential for broad and unforeseeable application as that urged by the State (*Id.* at 234).

At the time of this writing, the last reported case (In re H., 78 Misc. 2d 412, 357 N.Y.S.2d 384 (Fam. Ct. 1974)) concerning compulsory school attendance had to do with neglect of parents who chose to educate their children at home rather than complying with the state's compulsory school attendance laws.

The parents, who were well-educated and held permanent certification to teach, provided what they believed was substantial evidence of many educational achievements by the home training. In fact, they contended that the home instruction was at least equivalent to what could have been obtained by attending the public school.

The Family Court, however, was not satisfied and accordingly declared the children neglected on account of nonattendance at school:

> The proof here shows a lack of consistent quality in subject instruction, if not an absence of instruction in some areas and it shows the absence of a systematic approach to the course of study of the branches specified in the statute and regulations. These instructions are not adequate and the program, viewed as a whole, constitutes an attempt to evade the Compulsory Education Law (*Id.* at 391).

§ 2.6. Regulation of pupil appearance.

Scores of court cases have been reported over the past decade as to whether school authorities could determine the state of pupil appearance against the wishes of the parents. The great majority of the cases refer to hair styles.

In the very first case reaching a court of record (*Leonard v. School Comm. of Attleboro,* 349 Mass. 704, 212 N.E.2d 468 (1965)) parents contended that a regulation which bars a student from attending classes solely because of length or appearance of hair is "unreasonable and arbitrary, since these matters are in no way connected with the successful operation of a public school." They further contended that "the challenged ruling is an invasion of family privacy touching matters occurring while he is at home and within the exclusive control of his parents" (*Id.* at 472-73).

The court refused to pass upon the wisdom or desirability of the school regulation, but nevertheless responded to the parent's contention by stating:

> So here, the domain of family privacy must give way in so far as a regulation reasonably calculated to maintain school discipline may affect it. The rights of other students, and the interest of teachers, administrators and the community at large in a well run and efficient school system are paramount. . . . the discretionary powers of the committee are broad, and the courts will not reverse its decision unless it can be shown it acted arbitrarily or capriciously (*Id.* at 473).

More than a hundred court cases regarding hair styles of boys have been litigated since *Leonard.* Approximately one half of the decisions have upheld the school regulations, whereas the other half have been in favor of the pupils and their parents who act *ad litem* in their behalf.

In general, punitive action against students for violating a hair style regulation is unconstitutional unless positive proof is given to show that it is: (1) disruptive (*Dawson v. Hillsborough County, Fla. School Bd.,* 322 F. Supp. 286 (Fla. 1971)); (2) unsanitary (*Turley v. Adel Community School Dist.,* 322 F. Supp. 402 (Iowa 1971)); or (3) dangerous (*Lambert v. Marushi,* 322 F. Supp. 326 (W. Va. 1971)).

In a case (*Pound v. Holladay,* 322 F. Supp. 1000 (Miss. 1971)) which summarizes much of the litigation regarding hair styles, a United States District Court found that: "The great majority of the cases are recent and for the most part stem from the holding of the Supreme Court of the United States in *Tinker*," a case which will be treated later in this publication.

Much to the relief of the judiciary and others, the hair style issue has ceased to be a significant issue for litigation. Long hair is generally accepted as proper throughout society, including the public schools.

The legal principles relating to the school board's discretionary authority governing hair styles, as judicially decided, are applicable to virtually every phase of pupil appearance, as well as all other aspects of pupil behavior.

§ 2.7. Curricular requirements.

Numerous court cases have evolved which question the right of the school over the parent in determining what studies the student shall be required to pursue. In an early Nebraska case (*State ex rel. Kelley v. Ferguson,* 95 Neb. 63, 144 N.W. 1039 (1914)) a legal principle denoting the school's limited scope of authority over the curriculum was established when the Nebraska Supreme Court ruled against a school board which refused a request of a parent to excuse his daughter from studying domestic science. In support of its ruling the court stated:

> The public school is one of the main bulwarks of our nation, and we would not knowingly do anything to undermine it; but we should be careful to avoid permitting our love for this noble institution to cause us to regard it as "all in all" and destroy both the God-given and

constitutional right of a parent to have some voice in the bringing up and education of his children ... (*Id.* at 1043).

A long period of litigation concerned the flag-salute requirement of the school program against the will of parents. The Jehovah's Witnesses protested the regulation because their religion forbids homage to the flag. In the first United States Supreme Court decision on the case (*Minersville School Dist. v. Gobitis,* 310 U.S. 586, 60 S. Ct. 1010 (1940)) it was held that schools could require the flag salute as a means of achieving a feeling of national unity. Justice Frankfurter, who delivered the opinion of the court, stated in part:

> The preciousness of the family relation, the authority and independence which give dignity to parenthood, indeed the enjoyment of all freedom, presuppose the kind of ordered society which is summarized by our flag (*Id.* at 600).

The second United States Supreme Court case (*West Virginia State Bd. of Educ. v. Barnette,* 319 U.S. 624, 63 S. Ct. 1178 (1943)) overrode the decision of the earlier *Gobitis* case, and prevails as the present legal principal in force today.

In substance the Supreme Court held that a school board, in compelling pupils to salute and pledge allegiance to the American flag, "transcends constitutional limitations on their power and invades the sphere of intellect and spirit which it is the purpose of the First Amendment to our Constitution to reserve from all official control" (*Id.* at 642).

The issue of compelling participation in religious exercises in the public schools against the protests of parents has been litigated many times. After rulings on the Bible-reading controversy by state and lower federal courts, the United States Supreme Court finally ruled against the requirement in *School Dist. of Abington Township, Pa. v. Schempp,* 374 U.S. 203 (1963). Justice Clark, who wrote the majority opinion, made the following classic statement:

> . . . it is no defense to urge that the religious practices here may be relatively minor encroachments on the First Amendment. The breach of neutrality that is today a trickling stream may all too soon become a raging torrent and, in the words of Madison, "it is proper to take alarm at the first experiment on our liberties" (*Id.* at 225).

A school's authority to determine the curricular activities in which a student must participate, by virtue of *in loco parentis,* was given a judicial setback in Illinois in 1975 (*Chilton v. Cook County School Dist. No. 207, Maine Township,* 26 Ill. App. 3d 459, 325 N.E.2d 666 (1975)).

In the instant case a school district was held liable for damages sustained by a fifteen-year-old freshman who was severely injured in an unsuccessful attempt to comply with a curricular requirement that "the trampoline course was required of all freshmen students without regard to any demonstrated ability or experience on the trampoline" (*Id.* at 668).

The defendant school district argued that the School

Code conveys broad discretionary authority to educators who "stand in the relation of parents and guardians to the pupils" and that "this relationship shall extend to all activities with the school program and may be exercised at any time" (*Id.* at 669).

In response to this argument, the court stated:

> . . . we note that the trial court refused to instruct the jury that the *in loco parentis* standard was applicable to the case at bar and that the trial court declared that the basis for its ruling on the point was its belief that Section 24-24 applied only to disciplinary situations. We agree, and we find that the cited section does not specifically outline a broader basis for a school's disciplinary and supervisory powers and does not make such broader basis a matter of state law (*Id.* at 671).

§ 2.8. Obsolescence of the doctrine.

Such tremendous changes have occurred in the size, administration and programs of our public schools that the applicability of the *in loco parentis* doctrine is indeed questionable today. Also, extension of the doctrine beyond its original stipulation "as may be necessary to answer the purpose for which he is employed" has detracted from its viability. Moreover, with the decreasing stability of family life in many homes today, the teacher cannot be certain that acting as a parent might act in treatment of the child would be for the welfare of the child.

That the *in loco parentis* doctrine has lost its

appropriateness in the schools of today is expressed by many legal authorities and writers. Excerpts from some of their writings follow.

(Edward T. Ladd, "Allegedly Disruptive Student Behavior and the Legal Authority of School Officials," 19 *Journal of Public Law* 209, 219-20 (1970).)

Our system of public schools was born and developed in the context of New England Puritanism. In the earliest days of our schools, teachers, parents and pupils knew one another outside the school as well as in it, and the concept of a delegation of power to act *in loco parentis,* borrowed from the relationship of parent to private tutor, had a certain obvious validity. At that time the good *parens* was typified by the stern, repressive father, and the powers of the community's elders to "correct" the young were viewed as educationally necessary, divinely ordained and subject to no legal restrictions.

. . . As a result of urbanization, the phenomenal growth in school enrollments and, to a lesser extent, school consolidation in rural areas, some school districts and even some individual schools have come to embrace thousands of persons and to have budgets in the millions. These systems require specially trained administrators and complicated, formal provisions for control of the behavior of their members. For reasons not of concern here, they tend to have exceptionally bad channels of communication and exceptionally broad spans of control, so that every significant initiative from below threatens to be disruptive (*Id.* at 219-20).

(William L. Youngblood, "Recent Decisions," 44 *Mississippi Law Journal* 550-55 (1973).)

At common law the teacher had the right to administer corporal punishment based on the doctrine of *in loco parentis* which defined the teacher's authority as a partial delegation of parental authority. The rationale behind this doctrine is that in school discipline the teacher stands in place of the parent and has the right to use reasonable physical punishment to obtain the child's obedience. A more recent development of the law holds that the duty to maintain classroom discipline is necessary to the educational process and that the teacher has authority, independent of parental authority, to punish in all situations directly affecting school order (*Id.* 550-51).

When school enrollments were small and teachers could build personal relationships, the *in loco parentis* doctrine was feasible. But as a result of the phenomenal growth in school enrollments, some schools have exceptionally bad communication channels and broad spans of student control. This bureaucratic environment makes the *in loco parentis* doctrine inapplicable to many of today's modern school systems . . . (*Id.* at 554).

(William G. Buss, "Procedural Due Process for School Discipline," 119 *University of Pennsylvania Law Review* 545-641 (1971).)

Furthermore, although many teachers obviously care deeply about their students, the student-teacher relationship is significantly different from the parental one. In the modern school setting, the teacher does not and perhaps cannot have an individual, parent-like concern for the child's welfare. A close home-school community that might bring the teacher within the ambit of family trust rarely develops (*Id.* at 560).

When the sanction in question is exclusion from school, the doctrine of in loco parentis seems a peculiarly inappropriate justification for refusing to hear a student's plea for fundamental due process. Parents cannot take disciplinary action parallel to excluding a student from school, for they generally have a state-imposed duty to support and care for their children. Nevertheless, the school's authority in loco parentis has sometimes been offered as a justification for allowing expulsion without a hearing, and even when not explicitly advanced, the doctrine looms hazily in the background (*Id.* at 561).

(Thomas A. Gunn, "In Loco Parentis and Due Process: Should These Doctrines Apply to Corporal Punishment?" 26 *Baylor Law Review* 678-86 (1974).)

During the early period of our educational system, the doctrine of *in loco parentis* was a viable theory upon which the use of corporal punishment was based. As long as the relationship between parent and teacher was consensual, the parent controlled the use of corporal punishment by selection of the person who would hold disciplinary control over his child. Also, the parent could terminate the selection if he became dissatisfied with the teacher. But, when a parent sends a child to school because the law so directs, he delegates no such power to the teacher. To suggest that the parent delegates unrestricted power, especially when he objects to corporal punishment, is a questionable proposition. A closer examination of the doctrine of *in loco parentis* is mandated in order to determine its current viability as a justification for corporal punishment (*Id.* at 679).

. . . However valid the concept of *in loco parentis* may have once been, such validity has now ceased. No longer should a Latin phrase continue to vest such broad discretion in school authorities. The recognition that parents are possessed of a fundamental right, and indeed an obligation, to bring up their children as they see fit, mandates that parental rights take precedence over a doctrine that is no longer viable (*Id.* at 685).

(W. Roderick Bowdoin, "Balancing *In Loco Parentis* and the Constitution: Defining the Limits of Authority over Florida's Public High School Students," 26 *University of Florida Law Review* 271-88 (1974).)

While this outline of *in loco parentis* presents the two sides of the doctrine and the qualifications on each, modern decisions involving school authority must be viewed in light of the cultural changes in the United States, which have produced different attitudes regarding the student's legal character. Totalitarian authority granted to the schools in earlier cases has given way to a new concept of student rights, and students have been recognized by the Supreme Court as "persons under our constitution." The natural consequence of this new approach is a clash between students' asserted constitutional rights and the *in loco parentis* doctrine . . . (*Id.* at 274).

(Ralph D. Mawdsley, "In Loco Parentis: A Balancing of Interests," 61 *Illinois Bar Journal* 638-46 (1973).)

At least one school administrator believes the doctrine of *in loco parentis* is "alive and thriving." He admits the doctrine has been traditionally limited to student discipline cases but has been expanded to include a balancing of interests of the home and school. He claims that "although *in loco parentis* is not always mentioned as a court's reason for its decision, the basic philosophy of the doctrine is evident in a wide variety of different cases."

In concluding his argument, he states:

> In conclusion, *in loco parentis* is not a dead doctrine; it is in fact a doctrine that is alive and thriving. The concept has undergone an evolution from the simple delegation concept to an expanded concept involving the total family-school relationship. . . . The current interest in student rights has not pronounced the death knell of *in loco parentis;* rather there has been largely a shift of proof to the school to show that its regulations bear a direct relationship to disruption. Once the school has been able to satisfy the minimal obligations of the burden of proof, the regulation, or disciplinary action, has usually been sustained. According to the most recent case law granting of substantive and procedural rights to students has not eroded the relationship between the parents in the home and the school; these student rights have furnished a

modicum of protection for the student vis-a-vis the school authorities, but the courts still recognize that the limitation of these student rights is permissible because of *in loco parentis* (*Id.* at 644-45).

Chapter 3

DUE PROCESS AND SCHOOL DISCIPLINE

§ 3.1. Constitutional basis of due process.

The legal term "due process" stems from the Fifth and Fourteenth Amendments to the United States Constitution.

The Fifth Amendment provides in part: ". . . nor shall any person be . . . deprived of life, liberty, or property without due process of law."

The Fourteenth Amendment reads as follows:

> Section 1. All persons born or naturalized in the United States, and subject to the jurisdiction thereof, are citizens of the United States and of the state wherein they reside. No State shall make or enforce any law which shall abridge the privileges or immunities of citizens of the United States, nor shall any state deprive any person of life, liberty, or property, without due process of law, nor deny to any person within its jurisdiction the equal protection of the laws.

There are two types of due process, namely, "procedural due process" and "substantive due process."

> *Procedural due process* may be defined as the aspect of due process which relates to the

requisite characteristics of proc ʾings
looking toward a deprivation of life, liberty, or
property; procedural due process makes it
necessary that one whom it is sought to
deprive of such a right must be given notice of
this fact (that is, he must be given notice of the
proceedings against him), he must be given an
opportunity to defend himself (that is, a
hearing), and the problem of the propriety of
the deprivation, under the circumstances
presented, must be resolved in a manner
consistent with essential fairness. The idea of
procedural due process is reflected in the
statement that it is a rule as old as the law that
no one shall be personally bound until he has
had his day in court, by which is meant until
he has been duly cited to appear and has been
afforded an opportunity to be heard. Judgment
without such citation and opportunity lacks all
the attributes of a judicial determination; it is
judicial usurpation and oppression and can
never be upheld where justice is fairly
administered (16 *American Jurisprudence (2d)*,
Constitutional Law § 548, at 941-42 (1964)).

The guaranty of due process, viewed in its
procedural aspect, requires no particular form
of procedure. The due process clause of the
Fourteenth Amendment to the Constitution of
the United States does not control mere forms
of procedure in state courts or regulate
practice therein. The procedure by which
rights may be enforced and wrongs remedied
is peculiarly a subject of state regulation and
control. A state may regulate the procedure of
its courts in accordance with its own
conception of policy and fairness unless it

offends some principle of justice ranked as
fundamental, such as the requirements of
hearing and notice, or unless it is unreasonable
or arbitrary (*Id.* at 943-44).

Substantive due process may be roughly
defined as the constitutional guaranty that no
person shall be deprived of his life, liberty, or
property for arbitrary reasons, such a
deprivation being constitutionally supportable
only if the conduct from which the deprivation
flows is proscribed by reasonable legislation
(that is, legislation the enactment of which is
within the scope of legislative authority)
reasonably applied (that is, for a purpose
consonant with the purpose of the legislation
itself). . . . To be noted at this point are the
general principles that substantive due process
assures by requiring, that laws will operate
equally, and it affords freedom from arbitrary
action. It has been said that protection from
arbitrary action is the essence of substantive
due process, and similarly, that, in substantive
law, due process may be characterized as a
standard of reasonableness.

The principle of due process of law had its
origin in England as a protection to individuals
from arbitrary action on the part of the Crown.
It has been said that in this country the
requirement is intended to have a similar
effect against legislative power, that is, to
secure the citizen against any arbitrary
deprivation of his rights, whether relating to
his life, his liberty, or his property. It is a
limitation upon arbitrary power and a
guaranty against arbitrary legislation,
demanding that the law shall not be

unreasonable, arbitrary, or capricious, and
that the means selected shall have a real and
substantial relation to the object sought to be
attained (*Id.* at 946-47).

Due process an elusive concept. What constitutes
"procedural due process" within the ambit of the
Fourteenth Amendment is difficult to define. In
Hannah v. Larche, 363 U.S. 420 (1960), the former Chief
Justice Warren said:

> "Due process" is an elusive concept. Its
> exact boundaries are undefinable, and its
> content varies according to specific factual
> contexts. Thus, when governmental agencies
> adjudicate or make binding determinations
> which directly affect the legal rights of
> individuals, it is imperative that those agencies
> use the procedures which have traditionally
> been associated with the judicial process. On
> the other hand, when governmental action
> does not partake of an adjudication, as for
> example, when a general fact-finding
> investigation is being conducted, it is not
> necessary that the full panoply of judicial
> procedures be used. Therefore, as a
> generalization, it can be said that due process
> embodies the differing rules of fair play, which
> through the years, have become associated
> with differing types of proceedings. Whether
> the Constitution requires that a particular
> right obtain in a specific proceeding depends
> upon a complexity of factors. The nature of the
> alleged right involved, the nature of the
> proceeding, and the possible burden on that
> proceeding are all considerations which must
> be taken into account (*Id.* at 442).

§ 3.2. Impact of In re Gault.

Many of the early court cases invoking due process in the consideration of pupil discipline dealt mainly with *substantive* due process. In more recent years, especially after the United States Supreme Court decision on a much publicized case (*In re Gault,* 387 U.S. 1 (1967)), the *procedural* due process has come into sharper focus. Therefore this section of Chapter 3 will be confined to a discussion of that precedential case.

Background of the case. Gerald Gault, a 15-year-old boy, was arrested because of an alleged obscene telephone call to a neighbor. As a consequence he was immediately placed in a children's detention home. His parents, who were both at work away from home at the time, were not notified of their son's arrest.

On the day following Gerald's arrest, a probation officer filed a juvenile delinquency petition, void of any statement of facts, but merely a general recital to the effect that Gerald Gault was a "delinquent minor." The petition was not served on the Gaults before the hearing which was held in the chamber of the juvenile court judge. Gerald, his mother, and his oldest brother were present at this hearing, but, significantly, the neighbor who supposedly received and reported the obscene telephone call was not present at the hearing. Moreover, an account of what took place at the hearing was not recorded in any way.

After considerable conflicting testimonies, Gerald and his parents attended another hearing, at which the neighbor was again absent. At this meeting the judge merely glanced at a probation officer's referral report and immediately committed Gerald, as a juvenile delinquent, to the Arizona State Industrial School for the period of his minority which would have been for *six years,* since he was then just 15 years of age. The discriminatory injustice of the sentence is indicated by the fact that an adult convicted of the same offense would, under the Arizona Criminal Code, be subject to a maximum punishment of only a $50 fine or imprisonment for not more than *two months.*

Court sequence. Following the sentence imposed upon Gerald, his parents filed a petition for habeas corpus in the Arizona Supreme Court, which then ordered that the matter be heard by the Superior Court of Maricopa County. This court promptly dismissed the petition for habeas corpus and removed Gerald to the Arizona Industrial School.

On appeal the Supreme Court of Arizona affirmed the denial of habeas corpus, thereby upholding the action of the juvenile court. The Supreme Court of Arizona upheld the constitutionality of the Arizona Juvenile Code in that it is to read impliedly implementing the due process concept — concluding that the proceedings ending in the commitment of Gerald Gault did not offend those requirements.

The case was appealed again and finally carried to the United States Supreme Court, where on May 15, 1967, the High Court *reversed* the opinion of the Supreme Court of Arizona. In its review of the case, the United States Supreme Court gave primary consideration to whether a juvenile is a "delinquent" merely as a result of alleged misconduct on his part, with the consequence that he could be committed to a state institution.

Selected excerpts from the U. S. Supreme Court's opinion. Since the report of the court's opinion is exceptionally long (81 pages), only several of the most pertinent comments of the court are quoted in this publication. However, those who are interested in the limitations of the juvenile court system will be benefited by reading the entire majority, concurring and dissenting opinions. Moreover, numerous publications elaborate on the future of juvenile courts as a result of the United States Supreme Court decision. One of the most noteworthy and illuminating is ("Gault: What Now In The Juvenile Court?" *Institute of Continuing Legal Education,* Ann Arbor, Michigan (1968)). Ten legal authorities each contributed a chapter to the book.

Pertinent selected excerpts from the *Gault* opinion follow:

> From the inception of the juvenile court systems, wide differences have been tolerated — indeed insisted upon — between the procedural rights accorded to adults and those of juveniles. In practically all jurisdictions there are rights granted to adults which are withheld from juveniles. In addition to the specific problems involved in the present case, for example, it has been held that the juvenile is not entitled to bail, to indictment by grand jury. It is frequent practice that rules governing the arrest and interrogations of adults by the police are not observed in the case of juveniles (*Id.* at 14).

. . . We confront the reality of that portion of the Juvenile Court process with which we deal in this case. A boy is charged with misconduct. The boy is committed to an institution where he may be restrained of liberty for years. It is of no constitutional consequence — and of limited practical meaning — that the Institution to which he is committed is called an Industrial School. The fact of the matter is that, however euphemistic the title, a "receiving home" or an "industrial school" for juveniles is an institution of confinement in which the child is incarcerated for a greater or lesser time. His world becomes "a building with whitewashed walls, regimented routine and institutional hours. . . ." Instead of mother and father and sisters and brothers and friends and classmates, his world is peopled by guards, custodians, state employees, and "delinquents" confined with him for anything from waywardness to rape and homicide.

In view of this, it would be extraordinary if our Constitution did not require the procedural regularity and the exercise of care implied in the phrase "due process." Under our Constitution, the condition of being a boy does not justify a kangaroo court (*Id.* at 27-28).

We conclude that the Due Process Clause of the Fourteenth Amendment requires that in respect of proceedings to determine delinquency which may result in commitment to an institution in which the juvenile's freedom is curtailed, the child and his parents must be notified of the child's rights to be represented by counsel, that counsel will be appointed to represent the child (*Id.* at 41).

For the reasons stated, the judgment of the Supreme Court of Arizona is reversed and the cause remanded for further proceedings not inconsistent with this opinion (*Id.* at 59).

Since many persons might agree with the logic presented by Justice Stewart in his dissent to the majority opinion, brief excerpts are extracted from his dissenting opinion:

> The Court today uses an obscure Arizona case as a vehicle to impose upon thousands of juvenile courts throughout the nation restrictions that the Constitution made applicable to adversary criminal trials. I believe the Court's decision is wholly unsound as a matter of constitutional law, and sadly unwise as a matter of judicial policy.
>
> Juvenile proceedings are not criminal trials. They are not civil trials. They are simply not adversary proceedings. Whether treating with a delinquent child, a neglected child, a defective child, or a dependent child, a juvenile proceeding's whole purpose and mission is the very opposite of the mission and purpose of a prosecution in a criminal court. The object of the other is conviction and punishment for a criminal act (*Id.* at 78-79).
>
> A State in all its dealings must, of course, accord every person due process of law. And due process may require that some of the same restrictions which the Constitution has placed upon criminal trials must be imposed upon juvenile proceedings. For example, I suppose

> that all would agree that a brutally coerced confession could not constitutionally be considered in a juvenile court hearing. But it surely does not follow that the testimonial privilege against self-incrimination is applicable in all juvenile proceedings. Similarly, due process clearly requires timely notice of the purpose and scope of any proceedings affecting the relationship of parent and child. . . . But it certainly does not follow that notice of a juvenile hearing must be framed with all the technical niceties of a criminal indictment (*Id.* at 80-81).

Although the main thrust of this landmark Supreme Court decision was on the limitations of juvenile courts, the greatest contribution for the purpose of this publication is that it presents guidelines for due process considerations for all cases concerning discipline of pupils, regardless of juvenile court involvements.

§ 3.3. Fundamental due process rights of youth.

In essence the *Gault* decision means that before a juvenile can be found guilty and penalized he must be accorded the same due process rights accorded adults, such as: (1) notice of the charges; (2) right to counsel; (3) right to confrontation and cross-examination of the witnesses; (4) privilege against self-incrimination; (5) right to transcript of the proceedings; (6) right to appellate review.

(1) *Notice of charges.* The specific notice of the offense charged must be given before the hearing to enable the juvenile and his parents to prepare a defense,

the sort of notice which would be constitutionally
adequate in a criminal proceeding (as was noted in the
Gault decision, this requirement was not met). No
specific length of notice is specified. However, if there
are several witnesses, and if a conflict over the evidence
is indicated, sufficient time for the defendant should be
allowed.

The notification of the charges is particularly
important where youth are involved in serious disciplinary cases, as emphasized in a Texas case (*Sullivan
v. Houston Independent School Dist.,* 307 F. Supp. 1328
(S.D. Tex. 1969)):

> The high school student perhaps even more
> than the university student needs careful
> adherence to concepts of procedural fairness
> and reasonableness by school officials. . . . As
> minors they occupy a different status under
> the law and often are too inexperienced or
> immature to know how to protect themselves
> against charges of misconduct. Parents or
> guardians have legal obligations to children of
> high school age and common sense dictates
> that they should be included in any disciplinary
> action against their children which could result
> in severe punishment. Indeed it may be even
> more crucial that proper written notice of
> charges be provided to parents for often they
> do not know what has transpired at school.
> When severe discipline is contemplated —
> either expulsion or suspension for a
> substantial time — the student and his parents
> should be given ample time before the hearing
> to examine the charges, prepare a defense and
> gather evidence and witnesses. And, it goes

without saying that the disciplinary official should endeavor to maintain a neutral position until he has heard all of the facts (*Id.* at 1343).

Inadequacy of a notice is exemplified in a Wisconsin case (*Keller v. Fochs,* 385 F. Supp. 262 (E.D. Wis. 1974)) where a civil rights action challenged a student's expulsion, alleging violation of due process because of inadequate notice of charges. The only semblance of a notice of charges was a letter written by the school principal containing such statements as "your son . . . continues to conduct himself in an irresponsible and disruptive manner," and "he has been deliberately defiant of reasonable requests by teachers," and "on three different occasions within the past few weeks" (*Id.* at 266).

With such meager information in the notice of charges, the court concluded that:

> without more in terms of approximate dates and at least some recitation of detail significant enough to identify the conduct to the plaintiff, do not comport with the due process requirement of adequate notice of the charges. Nor have defendants presented any evidence to the effect that plaintiff was informed, otherwise than by the letters heretofore discussed, of which conduct would be the subject of the board hearing. For this reason, the Court concludes that plaintiff's due process rights were violated. . . . The lack of adequate notice necessarily affects plaintiff's ability to prepare his defense and thus the meaningfulness of his opportunity to be heard (*Id.* at 266).

(2) *Right to counsel.* Judicial opinions are not in agreement as to whether a juvenile has a right to counsel in disciplinary cases. For example in a case originating in New York (*Madera v. Board of Educ. of City of New York, 386 F.2d 778 (2d Cir. 1967)) where a pupil was suspended for disciplinary reasons without affording the pupil and his parents the right to be represented by counsel, it was held that a child's liberty is not in peril merely because a lawyer was not present: "The right to representation by counsel is not an essential ingredient to a fair hearing in all types of proceedings" (*Id.* at 786).

The more prevailing legal principle, however, is stated by the Commissioner of Education in New York in a pupil suspension case (*In re Cuffee,* No. 7816, Sept. 18, 1967, Judicial Decisions of the Comm'r of Educ. and Formal Opinions of Counsel, Vol. 7, Official Edition. The State Educ. Dept., Office of the Counsel, Albany, 1968, pp. 60-65) when he remarked:

> Recent court decisions have indicated that administrative officers may unreasonably infringe upon rights which, had the minor been of age, would have been protected by safeguards in the form of a right to a full hearing with representation by counsel (*Id.* at 61).

> Being a minor, the pupil is entitled to be questioned by the local authorities in the presence of his parents, and at the parents' option, his attorney, who in turn must be given an opportunity to question the school personnel involved. In the context of today's society, to deprive a pupil permanently of a high school education is too serious an injury to the pupil, as well as potentially to society, to allow omission of basic safeguards of due

process of law in ascertaining the true facts on which such action must be based, if it is to be taken at all (*Id.* at 62).

(3) *Right of confrontation and cross-examination of witnesses.* Courts have differed with respect to cross-examination of witnesses as an absolute necessity for procedural due process of students in disciplinary actions. Even though an evidentiary hearing, with opportunity of asking probing questions which often uncover inconsistencies, lapses or recollection of bias, the majority of courts thus far have chosen to support the rule not requiring the opportunity of confrontation and cross-examination of witnesses. The rule is particularly appropriate when the "informer" may be a fellow student. For example, in a Tennessee case (*State ex rel. Sherman v. Hyman,* 180 Tenn. 99, 171 S.W.2d 822, *cert. denied,* 319 U.S. 748 (1942)) the court held:

Students should not be compelled to give evidence incriminating themselves or which might be regarded as detrimental to the best interests of the school. Every governing authority should impress upon all students their duty to protect the honor and integrity of the school. As to the right to meet his accusers face to face in an investigation of wrongdoing, we cannot fail to note that honorable students do not like to be known as snoopers and informers against their fellows, that it is most unpleasant even when it becomes a duty. In these circumstances they should not be subjected to a cross-examination and, as is often seen in a trial court, to their displeasure if not their public humiliation. It would be subversive of the best interests of the school, as well as harmful to the community (*Id.* at 826).

(4) *Privilege against self-incrimination.* In an article (John J. Albert, "Procedural Due Process in Secondary Schools," 54 *Marquette Law Review* 358-69 (1971)) the author states:

The right against self-incrimination is generally associated with criminal, not administrative matters. Nevertheless, students are faced with two potential situations where Fifth Amendment rights may be operative. The first is under circumstances where a student's prehearing statements are used against him although he was not apprised of their potentially incriminating character. . . .

The second potential situation involves a student charged with a crime who finds himself on the school disciplinary carpet before the disposition of the criminal matter. The student thus risks expulsion if he remains silent and risks prejudicing his chances of success in any subsequent criminal proceedings if he speaks. . . (*Id.* at 365).

Turning back to *Gault* (387 U.S. 1), Justice Fortas, who portrayed the majority opinion of the Court, made the following comments pertaining to the right against self-incrimination:

The privilege against self-incrimination is, of course, related to the question of the

safeguards necessary to assure that
admissions or confessions are reasonably
trustworthy, that they are not the mere fruits
of fear or coercion, but are reliable expressions
of the truth. . . .

It would indeed be surprising if the privilege
against self-incrimination were available to
hardened criminals but not to children. The
language of the Fifth Amendment, applicable
to the States by operation of the Fourteenth
Amendment, is unequivocal and without
exception (*Id.* at 47).

In fact, evidence is accumulating that
confessions by juveniles do not aid in
"individualized treatment," as the court below
put it, and that compelling the child to answer
questions, without warning or advice as to his
right to remain silent, does not serve this or
any other good purpose. . . . it seems probable
that where children are induced to confess by
"paternal" urgings on the part of officials and
the confession is then followed by disciplinary
action, the child's reaction is likely to be hostile
and adverse — the child may well feel that he
has been led or tricked into confession and that
despite his confession, he is being punished (*Id.*
at 51-52).

We conclude that the constitutional privilege
against self-incrimination is applicable in the
case of juveniles as it is with respect to adults.
. . . If counsel was not present for some
permissible reason when an admission was
obtained, the greatest care must be taken to
assure that the admission was voluntary, in the
sense not only that it was not coerced or
suggested, but also that it was not the product

of ignorance of rights or of adolescent fantasy, fright or despair (*Id.* at 55).

§ 3.4. Limited applicability of due process rights in pupil disciplinary cases.

Following the *Gault* decision, in virtually every instance in which disciplinary action is taken against a pupil, the question arises as to whether due process has been afforded the pupil. In fact some courts and many school officials become annoyed with the claims of light disciplinary action taken in minor cases without complete conformance to *all* the rights of due process enumerated in the *Gault* opinion.

Consequently strict application of due process rights for pupils of all ages and for all offenses is receiving judicial scrutinization and criticism. A lower court case in Florida (*Conyers v. Pinellas County Bd. of Public Instruction,* Fla. Cir. Ct. No. 16, 634, 1969, p. 1) is in point where the issue was "whether the public schools must accord due process of law — charges, notice of hearing, time to prepare for hearing, confrontation of witnesses, appeal, stay pending appeal — in enforcing the school regulations respecting hair length" (*Id.* at 1).

The judge in this case pointed out the difficulties which would be encountered by school officials if pupils were granted due process in all matters of school discipline:

> Consider the chaos in our public schools if we are to permit seven-year-olds and eleven-year-olds and fifteen-year-olds and seventeen-year-olds to demand notice, time to

prepare for hearing, confrontation of witnesses, stay of judgment, and appeal each time a school official charges one with violation of a valid regulation and proposed approximate action. . . .
Our public school authorities have had wished upon them much more than they have asked. This court will not impose upon them the impossible (*Id.* at 8).

Federal courts also frequently minimize the adherence to procedural due process rights for pupils charged with misconduct, as illustrated by a case arising in Connecticut (*Farrell v. Joel*, 437 F.2d 160 (2d Cir. 1971)) where a United States Court of Appeals held that:

. . . even though student was not given written notice of charge against her and was not afforded a hearing before an impartial official at which she could confirm and cross-examine any adverse witness as well as present a defense concerning punishment, where no constitutionally required purpose would have been served by more formal procedures, in that student admitted that sit-in in which she had participated disrupted school activity, that she knew she was violating a school rule by not leaving when told to do so, and that she knew she might be suspended and was prepared to accept result (*Id.* at 160).
. . . Due process does not invariably require the procedural safeguards accorded in a criminal proceeding. Rather, "[t]he very nature of due process negates any concept of inflexible procedures universally applicable to

every imaginable situation" (*Id.* at 162).

... Of course, as one approaches the center of the two extremes of major and minor discipline the line becomes shadowy, but the difficulty of drawing it does not eliminate the distinction between the two. Moreover, the general age level of the student group involved might affect determination of the constitutional issue. A "demonstration" in kindergarten, after all, is not the same as one in college (*Id.* at 162-63).

Finally, in cases of minor discipline particularly, parent, student, and administrator should remember that substitution of common sense for zealous adherence to legal positions is not absolutely prohibited (*Id.* at 163).

Although parents frequently claim due process rights have been denied where corporal punishment has been inflicted upon their child, the misconduct sometimes requires immediate measures without first resorting to formal due process procedures.

In a case originating in New Mexico (*Sims v. Board of Educ. of Independent School Dist. No. 22,* 329 F. Supp. 678 (D.N.M. 1971)) the court stated:

This Court knows of no law which establishes the right of a school pupil to formal notice, hearing or representation, before corporal punishment may be inflicted by school authorities. We find no reported case so holding and counsel have cited none. This Court takes judicial notice that the purposes to be served by corporal punishment would be long since passed if formal notice, hearing and representation were required (*Id.* at 683).

§ 3.5. Suggested standard to follow.

A professor of school administration at Temple University presents a practical summation of the due process issue in an article (H. C. Hudgins, Jr., "The Discipline of Secondary School Students and Procedural Due Process: A Standard," 7 *Wake Forest Law Review* 32-48 (1970)), which reads in part as follows:

> Since schools first became public enterprises, the courts have given school authorities considerable latitude in managing student conduct. Moreover, judges have repeatedly reaffirmed that they have no intention of usurping the authority of boards of education and local administrators. The action that officials take against students must be consistent, however, with statutes and the common law. The old standard that courts will not interfere with school officials unless they have acted arbitrarily, capriciously, or unreasonably has given way to a new standard, that of insuring that individuals will be accorded due process rights. A student does not surrender his constitutional rights while at school. The United States Supreme Court stated this explicitly in protecting student speech in *Tinker* when the majority stated that one's rights do not stop at the schoolhouse gate.
>
> While insuring these rights, school administrators must also see that student behavior is maintained and that the integrity of the schools is preserved. The school building

and personnel must be protected from students who would otherwise disrupt or impair the educational program. In order to provide such protection, administrators have the responsibility for setting standards of behavior and for insuring that these standards are met. When student behavior is inconsistent with the school's objectives and policies, then the administration must deal with the offender.

In minor offenses the matter may be and often is resolved very easily by the student assuring his principal that the deviant behavior will be corrected and will henceforth conform to school rules.

In more serious incidents, a hearing may be necessary to establish if a pupil has been incorrigible and should be disciplined. If the behavior would necessitate that the student be removed from school, then there becomes a burden for the administrator to insure that the accused offender be accorded procedural due process rights. The extent to which these rights will be observed will be dictated by the gravity of the offense and punishment that is to follow (*Id.* at 45-46).

Chapter 4

ADMINISTRATION OF CORPORAL PUNISHMENT

§ 4.1. Statutory authority to administer corporal punishment.

Corporal punishment is generally conceived as intentional infliction of physical pain subsequent to misconduct for the purpose of deferring future misconduct. It came into use with the beginning of American education — long before *public* education was prevalent. It was based upon the common law, with the concept that the teacher stands *in loco parentis* in disciplinary matters. (This is treated in detail in Chapter 2 of this publication.)

With the advent of the *public* school system, and, especially, with the statutory provisions for compulsory school attendance, the application of *in loco parentis* as a right for a teacher to impose physical force upon a pupil as a means of maintaining discipline came into question. Some parents and school personnel favored the use of corporal punishment; whereas others opposed it. All were concerned with respect to its legality. Consequently many of the states enacted legislation defining authorization or prohibition of corporal punishment as a disciplinary practice in public schools.

An authentic research investigation on the issue was conducted by Vernon in 1968 (Thomas Edward Vernon, "Legality and Propriety of Disciplinary Practices in the Public Schools," unpublished Ed. D. Dissertation, Department of Education, Duke University, 1968). In a chapter dealing with the legality of corporal punishment, Vernon tabulates the statutory references to corporal punishment as found in the state statutes in 1967. He found that:

> Twenty-five states currently have specific statutes in their legal codes with regard to the administering of corporal punishment to pupils by school personnel while acting in their professional capacities. Twenty-four of these twenty-five states in one or more statutes authorize the teacher as the administrator to inflict corporal punishment, justify the use of force, or condone necessary and reasonable physical punishment of students in their charge. Only one of the states, New Jersey, has a statute which denies the use of corporal punishment to members of the school hierarchy. The twenty-five other states and the District of Columbia have no statutes concerning the practice, neither in particular nor by implication (*Id.* at 17-21).

In discussing the statutory limitations of corporal punishment, Vernon states:

> One state, Hawaii, implies the legitimacy of the punishment. It does so in this manner: "Any teacher may administer necessary and reasonable punishment upon any pupil while in attendance at school, and shall not in any way be responsible therefore."

Three states, Illinois, Pennsylvania, and West Virginia, do not specifically authorize corporal punishment by law. Instead, they have laws which state, as in the words of the Illinois statute with regard to teachers and other certified educational employees, that: "In all matters relating to the discipline in and conduct of the schools and the school children, they stand in relation of parents and guardians to the pupils. This relationship shall extend to all activities connected with the school program and may be exercised at any time . . . in the absence of their parents or guardians."

Oklahoma also has this type of statute. It is in addition to the one authorizing corporal punishment.

The remaining eight states, Arizona, Louisiana, Minnesota, New York, North Dakota, Texas, Washington, and Wisconsin, consider the use of physical force, "but not deadly physical force," upon another person as justifiable and not criminal under circumstances of a teacher entrusted with the care and supervision of a minor when and to the extent that he reasonably believes it necessary to maintain discipline. A statute of the state of North Dakota is typical of this category of law. It is part of the penal code and declares: "To use or attempt to offer to use force or violence upon or toward the person of another is not unlawful in the following cases: . . . when committed by a . . . teacher, in the exercise of a lawful authority to restrain or correct his . . . pupil, if the restraint or

correction has been rendered necessary by the
misconduct of such . . . pupil, or by his refusal
to obey the lawful command of such . . .
teacher, and the force or violence used is
reasonable in manner and moderate in degree
. . ." (*Id.* at 22-23).

There have not been many changes in statutory
provisions for corporal punishment since Vernon's
study — the main one being that Massachusetts has
joined New Jersey by statutorily prohibiting corporal
punishment in the schools.

The *New Jersey* statutory prohibition of corporal
punishment in the schools is stated as follows: "No
person employed or engaged in a school or educational
institution, whether public or private, shall inflict or
cause to be inflicted corporal punishment upon a pupil
attending such school or institution . . ." (New Jersey
Stat. Ann., 18A:6-1, p. 77 (1968)).

It may be noted that the New Jersey provision is
broadly inclusive in that it applies to *private* as well as
public schools, and at all grade levels.

The *Massachusetts* statute was enacted five years
later, with the following provision: "The power of the
school committee or of any teacher or other employee
or agent of the school committee to maintain discipline
upon school property shall not include the right to inflict
corporal punishment upon any pupil" (Mass. Gen. Laws
Ann., ch. 71, § 37G, 1974 Cum. Supp.).

According to a Report of the Task Force on "Corporal
Punishment," published by the NEA in 1972, it is
revealed that, in addition to the two states prohibiting

corporal punishment, as stated above, it is banned "by state school board policy in Maryland" as well as in a number of large cities.

The Report states further that thirteen states specifically permit corporal punishment, while in other states the teacher is given the same authority as the parent to discipline the child, or is simply authorized to maintain order and discipline (p. 24).

In addition, the Report of the Task Force of the NEA proposed a "Model Law Outlining Corporal Punishment" in which the phrasing was quite similar to that mentioned in the prohibitory laws of New Jersey and Massachusetts, but, also, suggested that it may be applied when reasonable and necessary under the qualifying circumstances:

> (1) to protect himself, the pupil or others from physical injury;
> (2) to obtain possession of a weapon or other dangerous object upon the person or within the control of the pupil;
> (3) to protect property from serious harm, and such physical restraint shall not be construed to constitute corporal punishment or bodily pain within the meaning and intendment of this section (*The Report,* p. 29-a).

§ 4.2. Limits of permissible corporal punishment.

Essentially, in order for corporal punishment to be legal, it must be reasonable in the eyes of the judiciary. Ever since the beginning of litigation on the issue, the courts have generally held that if corporal punishment is inflicted upon pupils it should (1) be in conformance with statutory enactment; (2) be for the purpose of correction without malice; (3) not be cruel or excessive so as to leave permanent marks or injuries; and (4) be suited to the age and sex of the pupil.

Early precedential cases. Despite the above guidelines, in early cases, the courts have differed as to what precisely constitutes legal and illegal corporal punishment. According to one line of decisions (*State v. Pendergrass,* 19 N.C. 365, 31 Am. Dec. 416 (1837); *Heritage v. Dodge,* 64 N.H. 297, 9 A. 722 (1887); *Boyd v. State,* 88 Ala. 169 (1890)), if no lasting or permanent injury is inflicted upon the pupil, the teacher will not be held liable for excessive punishment administered in good faith. A case which illustrates this principle is that of *State v. Pendergrass, supra,* which was decided by the Supreme Court of North Carolina in 1837. In rendering a decision in an action against a teacher for whipping a pupil so severely as to leave marks on the child's body for a number of days following the chastisement, the court expressed what it considered the proper rule of law:

> The line which separates moderate correction from immoderate punishment, can only be ascertained by reference to general principles. The welfare of the child is the main purpose for which pain is permitted to be inflicted. Any punishment, therefore, which may seriously endanger life, limbs, or health, or shall disfigure the child, or cause any other permanent injury, may be pronounced in itself immoderate, as not only being unnecessary for, but inconsistent with, the purpose for

which correction is authorized. But any correction, however severe, which produces temporary pain only, and no permanent ill, cannot be so pronounced, since it may have been necessary for the reformation of the child, and does not injuriously affect its future welfare. We hold, therefore, that it may be laid down as a general rule, that teachers exceed the limits of their authority when they cause lasting mischief; but act within the limit of it when they inflict temporary pain (*Id.* at 417).

Whether or not a teacher was actuated by malice in punishing a pupil is a matter of fact to be determined by the jury. In the case, *Boyd v. State, supra,* the Supreme Court of Alabama made the following distinction:

The more correct view, however, and the one better sustained by authority, seems to be that, when, in the judgment of reasonable man, the punishment inflicted is immoderate or excessive, and a jury would be authorized, from the facts of the case, to infer that it was induced by legal malice, or wickedness of motive, the limit of lawful authority may be adjudged to be passed. In determining this question, the nature of the instrument of correction used may have a strong bearing on the inquiry as to motive or intention (*Id.* at 269).

According to the second line of decisions, it is not sufficient to show that the teacher acted in good faith without malicious intent. If, in the opinion of reasonable men, the punishment was unreasonable and excessive, the teacher is guilty of assault, even though no malice was apparent. When there is doubt as to the reasonableness of the punishment, the teacher is usually given the benefit of the doubt. A decision by the Supreme Court of Vermont (*Lander v. Seaver,* 32 Vt. 114, 76 Am. Dec. 156 (1859)) exemplifies this line of reasoning:

> Hence the teacher is not to be held liable on the ground of excessive punishment, unless the punishment is clearly excessive and would be held so in the judgment of reasonable men. If the punishment be thus *clearly* excessive, then the master should be held liable for such excess, though he acted from good motives in inflicting the punishment, and in his own judgment considered it necessary and excessive. But if there is any reasonable doubt whether the punishment was excessive, the master should have the benefit of the doubt (*Id.* at 163).

Where moderation of punishment is a factor, the fact that an excessive beating may have a good effect on a pupil and the school does not relieve the teacher of liability. In a North Carolina case (*State v. Thornton,* 136 N.C. 610, 48 S.E. 602 (1904)) in which an angered teacher improved the discipline in the school by immoderately whipping a pupil, the court defined the following legal principle:

> The good effect the chastisement of the prosecutor had upon the discipline of the school was manifestly irrelevant. Suppose the defendant had grievously wounded the

prosecutor, or disfigured or maimed him, would such evidence be competent, and, if not in such a case why should it be if the punishment was excessive and inflicted maliciously? The law does not tolerate evil that good may come. A teacher by his very excesses may inspire terror in his pupils and thus subdue them to his will and authority, but the law will not excuse his cruel acts for the sake of good discipline in his school (*Id.* at 603).

Although a teacher is generally restricted to inflict only moderate punishment, in certain cases he may be allowed to employ more violent measures if the circumstances necessitate such action. Such was the case when a pupil, over seventeen years of age and larger in size and weight than the teacher, came to school armed with a pistol and threatened to shoot the teacher when he asked for the gun. The court upheld the teacher for using a club for the purpose of disarming the pupil and held that the punishment administered was not excessive in that particular instance. In rendering a decision in favor of the teacher, the court in *Metcalf v. State,* 21 Tex. App. 174, 17 S.W. 142 (1886), said at 143:

If the force used was not excessive, — and, in our opinion, it was not, — then appellant, instead of being punished, should be commended in his efforts to maintain obedience, not only to the rules of his school, but to the laws of the state. That the pupil should have been punished for carrying a deadly weapon into the school in violation of the rules is, we think, beyond question.

It may be noted by the foregoing case that, when a teacher acts in good faith without malice or ill intent, rather violent measures or punishment may be employed if circumstances necessitate such action. Significantly, however, the courts do not uphold a teacher for inflicting corporal punishment, regardless of the gravity of the case, if it be clearly shown that the teacher's intent is to inflict *immoderate* chastisement. Such was the reasoning of the court in a Texas case (*Dill v. State,* 87 Tex. Crim. App. 49, 219 S.W. 481 (1920)) in which a boy was acquitted on a charge of homicide after he had inflicted fatal wounds with a pocketknife upon a teacher who was about to administer immoderate punishment. The acquittal was based on the fact that the boy acted within his rights to protect himself from undue punishment.

Vacillating trends. As early as the 1940's it appeared that corporal punishment, as a mode of disciplining pupils, was to disappear from the schools. The tendency of public sentiment and the general tone of court decisions indicated its probable abolishment.

By 1960, however, there was indication that the pendulum was about to swing back toward greater "use of the rod" in the public schools. A case (*Indiana State Personnel Bd. v. Jackson,* 244 Ind. 321, 192 N.E.2d 740 (1963)) adjudicated in 1963 by an Indiana court suggested that the early-established legal principle that a teacher stands *in loco parentis* with respect to the disciplining of pupils may be predictive of renewed emphasis. In this case, involving the dismissal of a teacher for disciplining a pupil by striking her very lightly, the court made the following comment:

> The law is well settled in this state that the teacher stands in loco parentis to the child, and his authority in this respect is no more subject to question than is the authority of the parent. The teacher's authority and the kind and quantum of punishment employed to meet a given offense is measured by the same rules, standards and requirements as fixed and established for parents (*Id.* at 744).

Adherence to the *in loco parentis* doctrine, however, has not been as important a factor in the recurrence of ligitation on the issue as the legal principles growing out of interpretations of the Federal Constitution. Several of the later cases involve claims that corporal punishment is unconstitutional because of violation of the Eighth Amendment to the United States Constitution which prohibits ". . . cruel and unusual punishments. . . ."

Through the Fourteenth Amendment, the Eighth Amendment against cruel and unusual punishment has been applied to the official conduct of public school teachers and administrators in every state. A teacher's resort to corporal punishment has been held to constitute "punishment" within the meaning of the amendment and is therefore subject to constitutional restraints.

The Fifth Amendment to the Federal Constitution has also been a factor of consideration in corporal punishment cases because of the guaranty of due process rights, referred to in the preceding chapter of this publication.

§ 4.3. Recent court decisions — pro and con.

Although there have been relatively few cases during the past decade involving the legality of inflicting corporal punishment on pupils as a disciplinary practice, those which have been reported by courts of record since 1970 are discussed here in their chronological order.

(1) *Johnson v. Horace Mann Mut. Ins. Co.,* 241 So. 2d 588 (La. 1970).

Held legally impermissible:

This case involved an action for damages by a mother on behalf of her minor son and herself against the boy's teacher, principal and an insurance company. The mother claimed damages to her son resulted from "an excessive beating" administered with a stick by a physical education teacher.

Facts of the case indicated that because of disobedience at a physical education class, the teacher administered a whipping to the boy. Thereafter, the boy showed the principal of the school some marks on his backside as a result of the whipping. Also his mother took him to a physician who "detected multiple bruises on the body." However, there was "no evidence that the bruises were caused by any trauma other than the whipping."

The court found that: "No Louisiana statute or judicial decision is cited to us to establish the right of teachers to use corporal punishment" (*Id.* at 590).

In holding that the evidence indicated "the punishment was excessive and unreasonable" the court ordered that

> For pain, suffering and humiliation Jimmy will be allowed the sum of $1000.00. Although his injuries were not of a serious nature, the bruises took some time to heal, and were certainly not comfortable. Such a degrading experience as this public whipping has obviously caused Jimmy much discomfort, and is compensable (*Id.* at 593).

(2) *Ware v. Estes,* 328 F. Supp. 657 (N.D. Tex. 1971).

Held legally permissible:

This is not a case involving corporal punishment of a particular student, but rather, a class action challenging the constitutionality of rules and policy of the Dallas Independent School District which stipulated that: "Principals are authorized to administer any reasonable punishment, including ... corporal punishment ..." (*Id.* at 658).

The plaintiffs in this case charged

> that any corporal punishment administered without parental or student consent deprives them of their rights to due process under the Fourteenth Amendment because any utilization of corporal punishment is arbitrary, capricious and unrelated to any legitimate educational purpose. They also charge that this corporal punishment on its face, constitutes cruel and unusual punishment in violation of the Eighth Amendment as applied

to the States through the Fourteenth Amendment (*Id.* at 658).

The court admitted that, in rare instances, some of the seven thousand teachers in the Dallas schools may have abused the practice of corporal punishment but concluded that the policy itself was not unconstitutional, and added that:

> It is not within this Court's function, or individual competence, to pass judgment upon the merits of corporal punishment as an educational tool or a means of discipline. The wisdom of the policy is not the Court's concern. The only judgment made is that the evidence has not shown this policy to be arbitrary, capricious, unreasonable or wholly unrelated to the competency of the state in determining its educational policy (*Id.* at 659).

The Court pointed out that while the School District is not compelled to use corporal punishment, they are allowed to use it by a Texas statute which "has been construed as authorizing the school teacher to inflict moderate corporal punishment upon a pupil" (*Id.* at 660).

The decision of the district court was appealed to the Appellate Court where it was affirmed with the statement: "We are in agreement with the well considered memorandum opinion of the district court . . . and its judgment is confirmed" (458 F.2d 1360 (5th Cir. 1972) at 1361). On further appeal to the United States Supreme Court, certiorari was denied (409 U.S. 1027 (1972)).

(3) *Sims v. Board of Education of Independent School Dist. No. 22,* 329 F. Supp. 678 (D.N.M. (1971)).

Held legally permissible:

This case also involves a class action for declaratory injunctive relief against the policy and practice of corporal punishment in the schools of the district. The policy of the Board, set forth in the Teachers' Handbook, reads as follows:

> The most advanced educational theory opposes corporal punishment in the school. By and large, the administration of our schools supports this theory. However, it must be recognized that situations arise which can be considered exceptions to the rule. When other means have repeatedly failed, it may be necessary for the school authorities to administer a "spanking" to some recalcitrant pupil. When this is necessary, the punishment shall be administered by the school principal or if administered by the teacher it should be witnessed by the principal or his delegated representative in his absence. (*Id.* at 680).
>
> The complaint in this case alleges that "corporal punishment serves no legitimate educational purpose" and "tends to inhibit learning, retard social growth and force acceptance of an inferior class position upon the plaintiff and other similarly situated members of his class"; "subject him to further humiliation because of the public or semi-public character of the act as it is practiced"; and that "the psychological harm done plaintiff and other members of class by

the infliction of corporal punishment is substantial and lasting" (*Id.* at 680-81).

In upholding the right of the school to exercise discretion in inflicting corporal punishment, the court pointed out that:

Corporal punishment of pupils by teachers was practiced in the schools long prior to the adoption of the Fourteenth Amendment. It has continued to be practiced since the adoption of the equal protection clause. Neither the briefs of counsel nor the research of the Court has revealed a single reported case wherein such punishment was banned as invading the constitutional right of equal protection of students. The absence of a reported case is not without significance (*Id.* at 687).

Since the court could find nothing constitutionally or statutorily wrong, it stated in conclusion:

This Court cannot, under the applicable law, and would not if applicable law permitted the exercise of such discretion, substitute its judgment for the judgment of the defendants in the case at hand on what regulations are appropriate to maintain order and insure respect of pupils for school discipline and property. This Court will not act as a super school board to second guess the defendants. If acts violative of reasonable school regulations be not discouraged and punished, those acts can result in the disruption of the schools themselves. If our educational institutions are not allowed to rule themselves, within reasonable bounds, as here, experience has demonstrated that others will rule them to their destruction (*Id.* at 690).

(4) *Glaser v. Marietta,* 351 F. Supp. 555 (W.D. Pa. 1972).

Held legally permissible:

This case involves an action by a pupil and his mother to enjoin the school district from inflicting corporal punishment. In considering the case, the United States District Court held that:

> Corporal punishment of students under carefully controlled situations, in accordance with Pennsylvania school district administrative regulations as authorized by Pennsylvania statute, without excessive force was not in violation of constitutional rights of 12-year-old pupil to whom three medium paddle strokes were administered after assistant principal had determined through interrogation that such pupil was responsible for altercation in classroom (*Id.* at 555).

Before being punished, the boy stated that "his mother did not wish him to be paddled by school officials." However, when given the alternative of suspension, "he chose paddling."

The assistant principal, who administered the mild paddling, testified that "he did not use corporal punishment on a student when parents requested otherwise. He stated that he had not received any such prohibition" from the boy's mother (*Id.* at 557).

In support of its decision the District Court stated:

> After careful consideration, we hold to our

view that corporal punishment in the manner in which it is practiced in the Northgate School District is not violative of the Constitution insofar as the minor plaintiff is concerned. There was no excessive amount of force involved, the sanction is not used indiscriminately, and we do not find that use of corporal punishment *per se* is unreasonable under the circumstances (*Id.* at 557).

In conclusion, the court qualified its decision with the following statement: "Our ruling is that the School District may enforce its rules on corporal punishment except as to a child whose parents have notified the appropriate authorities that such disciplinary method is prohibited" (*Id.* at 561).

(5) *Simms v. School Dist. No. 1, Multnomah County,* 508 P.2d 236 (Ore. App. 1973).

Held legally permissible:

This case differs from most cases on corporal punishment, where beatings or spankings are involved, in that a teacher is charged with "assault and battery." The teacher was alleged to have wantonly shoved a pupil into a glass window, which resulted in injury to the pupil's arm. The teacher denied the allegation and contended that he was merely attempting to remove the pupil from the classroom because of disruptive actions.

A circuit court ruled in favor of the school district and defendant teacher, after which the case was appealed to the Court of Appeals where it was held that "the use of reasonable force by teacher to remove disruptive child from classroom did not violate any statute or violate state or federal constitutional prohibitions relating to cruel and unusual punishment" (*Id.* at 236).

After hearing much conflicting testimony, and reviewing proceedings in other cases, the court placed emphasis on the following annotation:

> It is a well-established rule of the law of torts that a teacher is immune from liability for physical punishment, reasonable in degree, administered to a pupil. The teacher is held (and in some jurisdictions is stated by statute) to stand in loco parentis, and to share the parent's right to obtain obedience to reasonable commands by force.
>
> But a teachers right to use physical punishment is a limited one. His immunity from liability in damages requires that the evidence show that the punishment administered was reasonable, and such a showing requires consideration of the nature of the punishment itself, the nature of the pupil's misconduct which gave rise to the punishment, the age and physical condition of the pupil, and the teacher's motive in inflicting the punishment . . . (*Id.* at 239).

Nevertheless, with respect to the plaintiff's argument that the trial court did not properly exercise its discretion, the Court of Appeals responded thusly:

> We do not agree. Such danger of untrustworthiness as may have existed due to the self-serving aspect of the declaration was largely obviated here because the declarant himself was also the witness through whom the exhibit was offered, and therefore subject

to cross-examination regarding all aspects of its authenticity, reliability and accuracy. . . . Clearly the court did not abuse its discretion here (*Id.* at 243-44).

(6) *Gonyaw v. Gray,* 361 F. Supp. 366 (D. Vt. 1973).

Held legally permissible:

The plaintiff in this case, a twelve-year-old pupil, was subjected to corporal punishment for admittedly sending a "dirty note" to a classmate.

A provision of the Vermont education law provides:

A teacher or principal of a school or a superintendent or a school director on request of and in the presence of the teacher, may resort to any reasonable form of punishment, including corporal punishment and to any reasonable degree, for the purpose of securing obedience on the part of any child enrolled in such school, or for his correction, or for the purpose of securing or maintaining order in and control of such school (*Id.* at 368).

The plaintiff challenged the validity of the statute for several reasons, one of which was that it

violates the Fourteenth Amendment due process requirement in its substantive aspect, is equally unavailing because "liberty," as guaranteed by the Fourteenth Amendment, does not guarantee the freedom of a school child from the reasonable imposition of school discipline (*Id.* at 369).

To this argument, the court responded:

> Of necessity, parents must delegate some disciplinary authority over their school children to the teachers who, among other things, are responsible for maintaining the order necessary to the educational process . . . (*Id.* at 369).

The plaintiff also contended that the statute was unconstitutional because of its "vagueness and overbreadth" to which the court replied:

> The mere fact that a statute vests an official with discretion in seeking legitimate objectives does not render that statute void for vagueness merely because the possibility exists that discretion may be abused. There may be borderline cases in which it is difficult to determine where the facts will fall, but such indefiniteness will not condemn the statute (*Id.* at 370).

Consequently it was held that the statute authorizing infliction of corporal punishment on pupils did not violate equal protection or due process clauses and was not void for vagueness and overbreadth.

(7) *Nelson v. Heyne,* 491 F.2d 352 (7th Cir. 1974).

Held legally impermissible:

Obviously there are differences of opinion regarding the legal discrepancy between administering corporal punishment in correctional schools and administering it in regular public schools. This issue was litigated in Indiana where severe corporal punishment was administered to pupils in a state correctional institution which offered academic and vocational programs.

The district court found that "the corporal punishment . . . constituted cruel and unusual punishment in violation of plaintiffs' 8th and 14th Amendment rights" (*Id.* at 354).

On appeal, the Court of Appeals affirmed the decision of the district court and remarked in conclusion:

> When a state assumes the place of a juvenile's parents, it assumes as well the parental duties, and its treatment of its juveniles should, so far as can be reasonably required, be what proper parental care would provide. Without a program of individual treatment the result may be that the juveniles will not be rehabilitated, but warehoused, and that at the termination of detention they will likely be incapable of taking their proper places in free society; their interests and those of the state and the school thereby being defeated (*Id.* at 360).

(8) *People v. DeCaro,* 17 Ill. App. 3d 553, 308 N.E.2d 196 (1974).

Held legally permissible:

In this case a teacher was faced with a situation where two sixth-grade brothers were directing vulgarities and defamatory statements at him both outside school with the apparent knowledge of other students and in the classroom with other students present, and where "the teacher could not have ignored the actions and attitudes of the two boys without forfeiting the respect of all the other students and creating a climate which would be detrimental to the educational process . . ." (*Id.* at 196).

Acting under the *in loco parentis* doctrine, and the state statute which "provides that teachers are responsible for maintaining discipline in the schools and gives them the same control over a student that a parent has" (*Id.* at 197), "the teacher acted within his authority and not in a malicious or wanton manner in allegedly spanking the boys with a twelve-inch ruler on their buttocks and the back of the legs, resulting in bruises . . ." (*Id.* at 196).

In holding for the teacher, the court concluded:

> Although we do not condone the application of physical force which is calculated to result in bruises, we do not believe the defendant's actions were malicious. The punishment was of a traditional nature applied to the traditional place and did not constitute a malicious or wanton disregard for the physical welfare of the boys even though it unfortunately may have resulted in bruises (*Id.* at 198).

(9) *Bramlet v. Wilson,* 495 F.2d 714 (8th Cir. 1974).

Held legally impermissible:

In this case public school students and their mother brought civil rights action against the school superintendent and members of the school board. They alleged that the students were victims of the board's policy which "fostered the infliction of corporal punishment as a means of discipline and that punishment as administered was cruel and unusual" (*Id.* at 714).

The Western District Court of Arkansas upheld the defendants in their move "to dismiss the complaint on the grounds that it did not state a claim upon which relief could be granted." The Court of Appeals, however, *reversed and remanded* the district court's ruling.

The Court of Appeals reasoned that infliction of excessive amounts of corporal punishment may constitute cruel and unusual punishment, and with respect to prospects of future inquiry, the court stated:

> In short, a threat of future injury arising from a policy challenged as offensive to the Constitution on its face and as applied is alleged here . . . no criminal statute valid on its face and valid as applied interjects a deterrent to future injuries. Thus, having alleged past infliction of corporal punishment, *excessive in nature,* and the threat of future injury, Bramlet has advanced facts which, if proven to be true, can sustain a right to injunctive relief (*Id.* at 718).

(10) *Ingraham v. Wright,* 498 F.2d 248 (5th Cir. 1974).

Held legally impermissible:

In reversing the opinion of a district court, the Fifth Circuit Court of Appeals discussed in considerable detail the constitutionality of the use of corporal punishment in Dade County, Florida. Although the Court found the board policies were not in themselves violative of the Eighth Amendment prohibiting "cruel and unusual punishment," it was disclosed that the disciplinary practices at Drew Junior High School were beyond those defined by board policy.

The Court expressed less concern as to whether the corporal punishment administered in numerous cases was limited to the Eighth Amendment than as to "how corporal punishment is actually administered."

The court stated:

> From the evidence presented, we cannot say that the actual practice of corporal punishment in the Dade County school system as a whole violates the Eighth Amendment. However, we conclude that the plaintiffs' evidence as to pattern, practice and usage of corporal punishment at Drew Junior High School was such that the trial court erred in dismissing . . . (*Id.* at 262).

> The system of punishment utilized at Drew resulted in a number of relatively serious injuries, and thus clearly involved a significant risk of physical damage to the child. Corporal punishment also creates a risk of psychological damage (*Id.* at 264).

> Taking into consideration the age of the individuals, the nature of misconduct involved, the risk of physical and psychological damage, and the availability of alternative disciplinary measures, we conclude that the system of punishment at Drew was "excessive" in a constitutional sense. The severity of paddlings at Drew, generally, violated the Eighth Amendment requirement that punishment not be greatly disproportionate to the offenses charged. Our review of the evidence has further convinced us that the punishment administered at Drew was degrading to the children at that institution (*Id.* at 264).

(11) *People v. Ball*, 58 Ill. 2d 36, 317 N.E.2d 54 (1974).

Held legally impermissible:

In this case, a teacher who paddled a pupil was convicted, by a circuit court, on a battery charge. On appeal, the Appellate Court reversed the circuit court's ruling. It was appealed further to the Supreme Court of Illinois where the ruling of the circuit court was upheld and that of the Appellate Court reversed.

The reported facts of the case indicate that the boy (age 11) was obstreperous and defiant on the playground where practices were held for the school's annual "Field Day" performance. Because of the boy's misconduct he was taken into the school building where another teacher was asked to step outside her classroom into the hallway to be an observer to the punishment to be rendered, which consisted of a paddling where the boy was struck on the buttocks 10 times with a paddle, 3 inches wide, and 20 inches long.

Immediately after dismissal, the boy went home and reported to his parents the paddling he had received. The family doctor took the boy to the hospital where the examining doctor

> testified that it was one of the most severe paddling cases he had ever observed. . . . The family physician testified that he ordered tranquilizers for the boy, who was emotionally distraught from the paddling. His mother also stated that the boy was very upset immediately after the incident and continued to become so whenever he saw the defendant (*Id.* at 55).

In finding the defendant guilty, the trial judge stated that while a teacher may administer "just and reasonable punishment — corporal punishment included" — in maintaining discipline in the classroom, the defendant in this case inflicted corporal punishment more severe than the boy's parents would have had a right to administer . . . The court further indicated that it did not intend to take the right of discipline away from a teacher who stands *in loco parentis* but rather to insure that such discipline is "just and reasonable" (*Id.* at 55-56).

The court added: "we think it follows that teachers should be subject to the same standard of reasonableness which has long been applicable to parents in disciplining their children" (*Id.* at 57).

(12) *Gordon v. Oak Park School Dist. No. 97,* 24 Ill. App. 3d 131, 320 N.E.2d 389 (1974).

Held legally permissible:

It was reported in this case that school pupils, by their mother, filed a suit against the school district, alleging that the district, through its teachers, board members and officials, "had maliciously and intentionally abused, attacked, hit, embarrassed, intimidated and harassed them" (*Id.* at 389).

The court, however, found that "The testimony, replete with conclusions, hearsay and other incompetent statements, including accusations against other schools, did not create an issue of fact that the conduct of defendant's personnel was malicious" (*Id.* at 393). Accordingly the court ruled: "Having considered the record, we find no facts which in any way tend to support plaintiffs' allegations of malice and injury on the part of defendant personnel. The trial court correctly found that there was no genuine issue of fact" (*Id.* at 394).

(13) *Roy v. Continental Ins. Co.*, 313 So. 2d 349 (La. App. 1975).

Held legally permissible:

This case typifies other recent cases where, in the absence of statutory prohibition, corporal punishment may be inflicted upon unruly students if *reasonably* applied. (The Louisiana statutes do not explicitly establish the right of a teacher to use corporal punishment but then neither do they prohibit same.)

In the instant case a teacher separated and reprimanded two boys for fighting. Later the boys resumed their fracas, whereupon the teacher grabbed them by their shoulders and threatened to take them to the principal's office. Upon release, Roy (the plaintiff) cursed the teacher, calling him a "god-damn son-of-a-bitch" and threatened reprisal by his father.

This aggravation prompted the teacher to apply a wooden paddle to the eighth grade student's posterior. Upon release the boy cursed the teacher again. Then "the teacher grabbed him, turned him on his knee and gave him three or four more swats with the paddle." (*Id.* at 351)

Although the 15th Judicial Court entered judgment in favor of the plaintiff, the ruling was reversed by the Court of Appeals of Louisiana.

In holding for the teacher, the Court defended its decision with the following well-stated comments:

> The use of corporal punishment or discipline by teachers apparently stems from the age old principle that a schoolmaster is regarded as standing in "loco parentis," or in the shoes of a parent while the child is attending school, and as a result shares in the right to demand and obtain obedience from the student. Thus parental authority has been deemed to be delegated to the teacher. Insofar as the type or form of discipline is concerned, it must be conceded that parents have the right to inflict corporal punishment upon their children, subject of course to the limitation of jeopardizing the health or safety of the child. This court is of the opinion that teachers likewise have this limited right. Without doubt, some children of school age are immature, undisciplined, rebellious, and have a self-serving inability to recognize the necessity for regulation. As a result disruptive conduct often occurs. A teacher has the duty of maintaining discipline and good order in our schools, in addition to being responsible for the progress, conduct, and education of our children. In order for these educators to discharge this duty and maintain orderly conduct of activities in the classroom and on the school grounds, we opine they must be given the means of enforcing prompt discipline, one such means being reasonable corporal punishment. A general rule to the negative, insofar as corporal punishment is

concerned would in our minds "encourage
students to flaunt the authority of their
teachers," and effectively shackle the teaching
profession at a time of rising disciplinary
problems in our schools (*Id.* at 353-54).

(14) *Baker v. Owen,* 395 F. Supp. 294 (M.D.N.C.
1975).

Held legally permissible:

This is the last case concerning legality of corporal
punishment reported at the time of this writing. The
case involved a mild paddling administered to a
sixth-grade student, which resulted in a suit, instituted
by Mrs. Baker, the boy's mother, claiming illegality of
the corporal punishment over parental objection.

Mrs. Baker argued that the North Carolina statute
which empowers school officials to "use reasonable
force in the exercise of lawful authority to restrain or
correct pupils and to maintain order" is unconstitutional
insofar as it allows corporal punishment over parental
objection.

The court was not convinced by Mrs. Baker's
argument as evidenced by its following statement:

It should be clear beyond preadventure, indeed
self-evident, that to fulfill its assumed duty of
providing an education to all who want it, a
state must maintain order within its schools . . .
So long as the force used is reasonable — and
that is all that the statute here allows — school
officials are free to employ corporal
punishment for disciplinary purposes until in
the exercise of their own professional
judgment, or in response to concerted pressure

from opposing parents, they decide that its harm outweighs its utility (*Id.* at 301).

Judge Craven emphasized that although teachers can paddle students they must follow three guidelines: (1) they must forewarn students of behavior punishable by paddling; (2) another school official must be present; and (3) parents must be furnished a written statement of the paddling on request.

The *Baker* case was appealed to the U. S. Supreme Court (96 S. Ct. 210) where on October 20, 1975, the Court affirmed, without comment, the decision of the lower court.

§ 4.4. Denunciation of the practice.

A sample of the educator's point of view on corporal punishment in the public schools is provided by Vernon in the report of his doctoral research on the "Legality and Propriety of Disciplinary Practices in the Public Schools," *supra* ch. 4:

> Corporal punishment is not manifestly educative. Its immediate purpose is to inflict pain. Its effectiveness is based on a psychology of fear and humiliation.... Administering corporal punishment usually falls within the scope of the individual teacher or administrator's authority. As such, its use tends to put him in an unfavorable light and possibly to destroy the respect held for him by the rest of the pupils. Its use may create a personal battle between the pupil and the teacher in which the pupil might act in self-defense, further complicating the punishment. On the other hand, punishment

inflicted may be completely ineffective in stimulating a sensation of pain. Older pupils might not mind it at all. When there is no fear or distasteful sensation, some could prefer the administration of corporal punishment as a quick alternative to other penalties such as suspension, or loss of privilege, or involvement of parents (*Id.* at 50-51).

Any form of punishment is a tricky teaching technique. Yet many teachers use it without thinking, offhand, almost as a matter of course. In reality the pain that is inflicted carries the full teaching load. Any contribution which the heart might add is undercut by the strong right arm (*Id.* at 51-52).

In his critique of the *Ware v. Estes* case, *supra*, in 44 *Mississippi Law Review* 550-55 (1973), William L. Youngblood states:

. . . In contrast to public opinion, experts in the field of education and child psychology have adopted the view that corporal punishment is a counterproductive means of achieving order in schools. B. F. Skinner, a widely recognized authority on child psychology, asserts that corporal punishment has many unfortunate by-products which may lead students to attack teachers, become drop-outs, vandalize school property, and when they become voters, refuse to support education . . . (*Id.* at 553-54).

With an understanding of the harmful effects of corporal punishment and an appreciation for the recently recognized constitutional status of students, the instant court should have found the use of corporal punishment to be violative of due process and the protection against cruel and unusual punishment.... If petitioned to review the question again, the Court must find the use of corporal punishment to be unlawful if justice is to be accorded to thousands of American school children (*Id.* at 555).

In a discussion of the *Sims v. Board of Educ.* case, *supra*, John C. Lillie writes in 50 *North Carolina Law Review* 911-17 (1972):

... The elimination of corporal punishment in areas other than education is indicative of the general attitude of society towards corporal punishment and relevant to the determination that corporal punishment violates the concept of dignity and the civilized standards of contemporary society.

There is also important judicial authority for the assertion that corporal punishment in secondary schools violates the eighth amendment. The case of *Jackson* v. *Bishop* [404 F.2d 571 (8th Cir. 1968)] is, for example, highly relevant, although the court in *Sims* declared *Jackson* to be distinguishable because it involved the infliction of corporal punishment upon Arkansas prisoners rather than upon students. In *Jackson,* Judge (now Justice) Blackmun stated that corporal punishment "offends contemporary concepts of decency and human dignity and precepts of civilization which we profess to possess." The broad characterization of corporal punishment as offensive to contemporary values cannot be ignored (*Id.* at 913).

Further criticism of administering corporal punishment in the public schools is cited by Peter S. Aron and Martin L. Katz in "Corporal Punishment in the Public Schools: *Murray v. Kerrigan*," 6 *Harvard Civil Rights — Civil Liberties Law Review* 583-94 (1971). They state:

> Corporal punishment has further dele- terious effects on children. Insofar as it relies on fear, it disrupts the learning process by repressing the natural tendency of children to explore. This fear may be channeled into agression against the teacher, against the school, or against society. At the extreme, juvenile delinquency may result. Finally, and perhaps most seriously, the use of corporal punishment may inhibit the development of self-criticism and self-direction in the child. Corporal punishment may drive students to concentrate their energies on conflict with the teacher instead of encouraging them to adjust to their classroom situation (*Id.* at 584-85).

Although the above comments are of a comparatively recent period of time, the administration of corporal punishment was judicially denounced over a century ago, as indicated by Judge Stuart's statement on *Cooper v. McJunkin,* 4 Ind. 290 (1853):

> In one respect the tendency of the rod is so evidently evil, that it might, perhaps be arrested on the ground of public policy. The practice has an inherent proneness to abuse. The very act of whipping engenders passion, and very generally leads to excess (*Id.* at 292).
> It can hardly be doubted but that public

opinion will in time, strike the ferule from the hands of the teacher leaving him as the true basis of government, only the resources of his intellect and heart. Such is the only policy worth of the state, and of his otherwise enlightened and liberal institutions. It is the policy of progress. The husband can no longer moderately chastise his wife; nor, according to the more recent authorities, the master his servant or apprentice. Even the degrading cruelties of the naval service have been arrested. Why the person of the school-boy, "with his shining morning face," should be less sacred in the eyes of the law than that of the apprentice or the sailor, is not easily explained. It is regretted that such are the authorities — still courts are bound by them (*Id.* at 292-93).

Judge Stuart's speculation that corporal punishment in the public schools might eventually be eliminated on the ground of "public policy" is nearing fruition. As of now, however, as indicated by the cases discussed in this chapter, it is still being condoned in many instances but — significantly — with increasingly strict limitations.

Chapter 5

EXCLUSIONARY PRACTICES: SUSPENSION—EXPULSION

§ 5.1. Nature and differentiation of the practices.

In general, school officials are granted considerable discretionary authority to formulate rules and regulations for pupil control. Although the formulated rules and regulations are not usually contested in the courts, the methods of their enforcement frequently are. The most common methods employed in the enforcement of rules and regulations governing pupil conduct are *corporal punishment*, which was discussed in the preceding chapter, and *suspension* and *expulsion* to be treated in this chapter.

Now, when secondary school students become obstreperous and unruly to the extent of obstructing the educational process, school personnel and officials are authorized and expected to remove such students from the classroom or school premises. Even here, however, the authority for removal is limited by statutes and judicial mandate.

The legal principle is firmly established that school

authorities may *suspend* or *expel* from school any student who disobeys a reasonable rule or regulation within statutory limits. With the alarming increase of student misbehavior in the public schools today, and the diminution of corporal punishment as a means of abating the misbehavior, school authorities often exercise their discretionary prerogative to employ the alternatives of suspension and expulsion.

It may be noted in reading the many treatises dealing with pupil discipline, and the increasing number of case reports by courts of record, that the terms "suspension" and "expulsion" are sometimes used interchangeably. There is, however, considerable difference in the legal meaning of the two terms. "Suspension" is generally an act of a professional member of the school staff, whereas "expulsion" is a prerogative of the school board. Suspension is usually for a short period of time, or until the pupil conforms to the rule or regulation involved, whereas expulsion is usually permanent or substantially so.

While suspension is generally conceived to mean only a temporary withdrawal of a student from school, the more severe method of expulsion implies permanence or at least a long period of time, such as for the remainder of a term or the current school term. Because of the recent United States Supreme Court ruling in *Goss v. Lopez* (to be discussed later in this chapter) involving suspension, it is questionable as to just what differentiation, if any, there will ultimately be as far as administrative procedures are concerned.

Sometimes when a student refuses to modify his

misbehavior to conform with the school rule or regulation, an intended short-term suspension could culminate in actual expulsion. Moreover, when a student's misconduct or disobedience is of such a grave nature that his presence is disrupting to the school and detrimental to the morale of the student body, suspension, or even expulsion, is likely to be judicially condoned.

§ 5.2. Statutory authority for suspension and expulsion.

The statutes are less specific in reference to suspension and expulsion than they are to corporal punishment. Nevertheless, all states have provisions in their statutes which specifically or impliedly authorize suspension and expulsion as permissible measures for dealing with recalcitrant and incorrigible students.

Vernon, *supra*, who scanned all the state statutes with respect to their application to the suspension and expulsion of incorrigible students found that:

> Forty-six of the states have enactments which specifically authorise the use of suspension or expulsion as measure for student control. Four of the states along with the District of Columbia fail to provide that specific authorization by making no statutory mention of either practice. Those states are Delaware, Georgia, New Mexico, and Utah. Simply because the five units have not enacted laws giving specific sanction to the subject measures does not imply that there is a lack of legitimacy for their use in those states, nor

does it imply that they are prohibited practices
(*Id.* at 76).

Thirty-three   of   the   forty-six   states
authorizing suspension or expulsion have
qualified that authority. The qualifications are
of two general classes: (1) qualifications which
provide an appellate system and designate a
higher authority to whom an appeal could be
directed and (2) qualifications which prevent a
permanent dismissal and which establish a
maximum time limitation on the exclusion
period (*Id.* at 86).

Those states which qualify their exclusion
measures with only an appellate provision are
sixteen in number.... There are only two
states which qualify exclusion authority with
a time limitation without specifying an
appellate procedure. They are Oregon and
Texas (*Id.* at 87).

Regardless of statutory provisions pertaining to
suspension, it is probable that many of them will be
negated as a result of the *Goss v. Lopez* decision. A
United States Supreme Court decision concerning
constitutional rights takes precedence over all state
constitutional or statutory provisions pertaining to
educational matters.

§ 5.3. Early judicial leniency toward administrative practices.

It is noteworthy that a half century ago the courts
placed virtually no limitations upon school boards'
discretion to suspend or expel a student for various
offenses — even minor ones. Outside of determining the

reasonableness of pupil dismissal, the courts refused to interfere with school-board actions.

In one of the earliest illustrative cases (*Pugsley v. Sellmeyer*, 158 Ark. 247, 250 S.W. 538 (1923)) the Supreme Court of Arkansas upheld expulsion of a student for violation of a rule against the use of cosmetics. The court's rationale for noninterference is expressed as follows:

> The question, therefore, is not whether we approve this rule as one we would have made as directors of the district, nor are we required to find whether it was essential to the maintenance of discipline. On the contrary, we must uphold the rule unless we find that the directors have clearly abused their discretion, and that the rule is not one reasonably calculated to effect the purpose intended, that is, of promoting discipline in the school; and we do not so find.
>
> Courts have other and more important functions to perform than that of hearing the complaints of disaffected pupils of the public schools against rules and regulations promulgated by the school boards for the government of the schools.... These directors are in close and intimate touch with the affairs of their respective districts, and know the conditions with which they have to deal. It will be remembered also that respect for constituted authority and obedience thereto is an essential lesson to qualify one for the duties of citizenship, and that the schoolroom is an appropriate place to teach that lesson; so that the courts hesitate to substitute their will and

judgment for that of the school boards which are delegated by law as the agencies to prescribe rules for the government of the public schools of the state, which are supported at the public expense (*Id.* at 539).

In another case (*Tanton v. McKenney*, 226 Mich. 245, 197 N.W. 510 (1924)) adjudicated just one year later, the Supreme Court of Michigan upheld suspension and expulsion of a student for various alleged "acts of indiscretion." The judicial attitude of the court is similar to that expressed in the preceding case, as is indicated by the following comment:

> The enjoyment of the right of attending the public schools is necessarily conditioned on compliance by pupils with the reasonable rules, regulations, and requirements of the school authorities, breaches of which may be punished by suspension or expulsion. Ordinarily the school authorities have the right to define the offenses for which the punishment of exclusion from school may be imposed, and to determine whether the offense has been committed, the limitation on this authority being that it must in both respects be reasonably exercised. . . . In the school, as in the family, there exists on the part of the pupils the obligation of obedience to lawful commands, subordination and civil deportment, respect for the rights of others, and fidelity to duty. These obligations are inherent in any proper school system, and constitute, so to speak, the common law of the school (*Id.* at 512).

One more case (*Stromberg v. French,* 236 N.W. 477 (N.D. 1931)) is cited to indicate the broad authority school boards possessed several decades ago in the suspension and expulsion of students without judicial nullification. The case grew out of a school board rule which stipulated that "any boy wearing metal heel plates on his shoes will be refused admittance to classes and will be suspended or expelled until the heel plates are removed." When taken to the Supreme Court of North Dakota it was "held that the rule in question was a reasonable one and that the board of education had the right to make and enforce it" (*Id.* at 478).

Even though the record disclosed that no exception could be taken to the fact that the boy was an excellent student, and that he violated no rule except that with respect to the wearing of metal heel plates, and then only because of parental direction. The Supreme Court attempted to support its decision upholding the board action thusly:

> ... It seems to us that even so his conduct amounted to insubordination. Any other construction put upon the term as used in the statute might result in an intolerable situation. No rule or regulation could be enforced, provided the parent directed the pupil not to observe it. So we hold that the action of Murray, though taken at the command of his parents, constituted insubordination within the meaning of that term as used in the statute (*Id.* at 480).

Although the leniency of the judiciary in considering school boards' actions of suspending and expelling students for misconduct is reflected mostly in early cases, there are still rare instances where the courts will not intervene, as will be noted in the following section of this chapter. Unless the boards' exclusionary actions are unreasonable or in conflict with due process rights, they are likely to be judicially condoned.

§ 5.4. Recent decisions upholding suspension or expulsion.

It would be beyond the intended scope of this project to discuss, or even cite, all the court cases reported on the issues of suspension and expulsion. Only a sampling of cases which are most representative and recent are treated in this chapter. This section refers to court decisions *upholding* exclusionary practices of school personnel and officials.

(1) *Tate v. Board of Educ. of Jonesboro, Ark. Special School Dist.,* 453 F.2d 975 (8th Cir. 1972).

Twenty-nine black students got up and left a pep assembly in protest of the playing of "Dixie." "After consulting with other school officials, the superintendent advised the students that the walkout action was deemed disruptive of the school program and they were being suspended for a period of five days for such action" (*Id.* at 977).

The plaintiffs argued that "their departure from the pep rally was symbolic action guarded from suppression by the Free Speech Clause of the First Amendment to the Federal Constitution" (*Id.* at 978). To support their argument they cited *Tinker v. Des Moines Independent Community School Dist.,* 393 U.S. 503, 89 S. Ct. 733 (1969).

The court rejected the argument, pointing out that in *Tinker* "the Supreme Court was dealing with direct primary, First Amendment rights akin to 'pure speech' " and not with "aggressive, disruptive action or even group demonstration," as in the *Tate* case (*Id.* at 978).

In conclusion the court stated:

> On this record we cannot say that the tune "Dixie" constitutes a badge of slavery or that the playing of the tune under the facts as presented constituted officially sanctioned racial abuse. Such a ruling would lead to the prohibition of the playing of many of our most famous tunes.
>
> ... The action taken by the school authorities obviously averted serious trouble and was not only practical but clearly and properly within the rights of the school officials if we are to have any discipline in our public schools. Court intervention could in such situations only serve to fan the embers of unrest. The court should never interfere except where there is a clear case of constitutional infringement (*Id.* at 982).

(2) *Tucson Public Schools, Dist. No. 1 of Pima County v. Green,* 17 Ariz. App. 91, 495 P.2d 861 (1972).

The Court of Appeals of Arizona upheld the school board's permanent suspension of a student whose conduct precipitated a disruption in the classroom. No question was raised concerning due process procedures. "The essence of the attack on the school board's ruling was that permanent expulsion was an abuse of discretion" (*Id.* at 862).

Although the court agreed that expulsion was too severe as a punitive measure, it refused to interfere with the board's discretionary authority in the matter. The rationale of the court's decision is expressed in its concluding comments:

> The terms "arbitrary, capricious and unreasonable conduct" so as to constitute a manifest abuse of discretion calling for judicial intervention means unreasoning action, without consideration and in disregard for facts and circumstances; where there is room for two opinions, the action is not arbitrary or capricious if exercised honestly and upon due consideration, even though it may be believed that an erroneous conclusion has been reached. . . . Since the school board had authority to mete out punishment, judicial belief that the punishment was too harsh does not warrant "mixing in." The question of reinstatement of a student who has learned his lesson must be left to the governing board of the school district and a *laissez-faire* policy must be observed by the courts (*Id.* at 864).

(3) *Linwood v. Board of Educ., City of Peoria, School Dist. No. 150,* 463 F.2d 763 (7th Cir. 1972).

The Illinois School Code provides that the Board of Education shall have the power "to expel pupils guilty of gross disobedience or misconduct, and no action shall lie against them for such expulsion. Expulsion shall take place only after the parents have been requested to appear at a meeting of the board, or with a hearing officer appointed by it, to discuss their child's behavior (*Id.* at 765).

Accordingly a child's mother was given written notice to meet with the board relative to a charge of the boy's gross disobedience and misconduct for allegedly attacking and striking other students. After a district court upheld the board in its expulsion of the pupil for a period of seven days, the mother sought reversal of the judgment on the grounds that the board's action was unconstitutional.

In affirming the holding of the district court, the Court of Appeals stated: "We are of the view that a suspension for so relatively a short period for reasonably proscribed conduct is a minor disciplinary penalty which the legislature may elect to treat differently from expulsion or prolonged suspension without violating a constitutional right of the student" (*Id.* at 768-69).

The court expressed the opinion that the due process in this case was not to be equated with one of a criminal or a juvenile court delinquency proceeding where all the formal procedures would be constitutionally required.

(4) *Betts v. Board of Educ. of City of Chicago,* 466 F.2d 629 (7th Cir. 1972).

This case did not actually pertain to suspension or expulsion but rather a transfer of a girl student to a different school because of gross misdeeds. The girl was charged with, and admitted, activation of three false fire alarms "necessitating evacuation of four thousand students and two hundred faculty members for five to seven minutes on each occasion and requiring the presence of three fire department vehicles and their personnel" (*Id.* at 631).

Mrs. Betts and her daughter challenged the constitutionality of the board's act in removing her from the school, which was "tantamount to expulsion," in that it violated the due process clause of the Fourteenth Amendment. The district court, however, disagreed, thereby upholding the board's punitive action. On appeal, the district court's ruling was affirmed by the Court of Appeals.

The court agreed that the girl's interest in continuing her education was within the purview of the Fourteenth Amendment's due process protection, but reasoned:

> As to what process is due, it is important that the plaintiff unequivocally admitted the misconduct with which she was charged. In such a circumstance the function of procedural protections in insuring a fair and reliable determination of the retrospective factual question whether she in fact activated the false fire alarms is not essential (*Id.* at 633).

(5) *Wise v. Sauers,* 345 F. Supp. 90 (E.D. Pa. 1972).

This case arose as a result of high school students wearing armbands bearing the words "strike," "rally," or "stop killing." School officials advised the students that they would be permitted to wear plain armbands but would be prohibited from wearing armbands with the words written on them. Most students cooperated by removing the armbands or changing to plain ones. Bennett Wise, however, refused to comply and was accordingly suspended.

In upholding the actions of the school officials, the court made the following and concluding statement:

> The temporary restriction by the school against the wearing of the armbands with the words "strike," "rally," and "stop killing" was not related to the suspension of "pure speech" or to the popularity or unpopularity of the ideas sought to be expressed thereby, or the administrators' view of the same. The restriction was related to the potentially disruptive situation at the school at that time. Dr. Sauers and his colleagues were interested in and had the responsibility to insure the continuing education and safety of all students. This Court will not now second guess their judgment. We feel that the limited restrictions imposed upon the students were reasonable and necessary. The refusal of a student to obey the reasonable requests in this case was insubordinate and unprotected activity (*Id.* at 93).

(6) *Edwards v. Jersey Shore Area School Dist.*, 7 Pa. Cmwlth. 636, 301 A.2d 116 (1973).

If the charge in this case had been based on corporal punishment instead of expulsion, the decision of the court would have been the same.

A confrontation between a student and a teacher developed when the teacher attempted to send the offending student to the principal's office because of disobedience and defiance. When the student refused to go to the principal's office as ordered, the teacher went to his seat, "slapped him, pulled him up and started pushing him toward the door." After some scuffling, the student retaliated by hitting the teacher in the face with the back of his hand. "The blow was sufficient to cut the inside of her mouth and she required medical attention" (*Id.* at 117). The school board suspended the boy and followed due process procedure by notifying the parents by letter and advising them of a hearing which was held.

A lower court refused to honor the charge that the action of the teacher amounted to unjustifiable assault and battery and accordingly upheld the board's action. On appeal, the Commonwealth Court affirmed the decision of the lower court with the following decisive statement:

> Certainly Edwards' actions amounted to "misconduct," and striking a teacher is clearly inexcusable conduct on the part of a pupil unless he is acting strictly in self-defense. The lower court found, and there is simple evidence on the record to support such a finding, that Edwards was not justified in striking Mrs. Cox under the circumstances here present. While the legislature has chosen to permit teachers the reasonable use of physical force in certain circumstances, it has not sanctioned the retaliatory use of physical force by a student. Nor can we. There are few, if any, actions by a student less justifiable than the striking of a teacher, and few, if any, which would constitute more appropriate grounds for suspension (*Id.* at 118).

(7) *People in Interest of K.P.,* 514 P.2d 1131 (Colo. 1973).

The student involved in this case was expelled from the Denver public school system as the result of assaults which he made on some of his fellow students. At the request of the principal, the school superintendent suspended the student for a period of five days which was later extended ten days to allow time for school authorities to complete a thorough investigation of facts. Later the length of suspension was ordered for the remainder of the school year.

During the investigation, procedural due process was strictly adhered to despite the fact that K.P. charged that he was denied the right to "compulsory process" on two occasions. The lower court disagreed and, on appeal, the Supreme Court of Colorado upheld the decision of the Juvenile Court in ruling the Board's action was valid with the following remark:

> We conclude that having waived both procedural safeguards, K.P. was not deprived of either compulsory process or the right to have witnesses sworn and, therefore, that his expulsion hearing was procedurally proper (*Id.* at 1134).

(8) *Gonzalez v. School Dist. of Phil.,* 8 Pa. Cmwlth. 130, 301 A.2d 99 (1973).

This case grew out of a complaint in equity seeking injunctive relief with respect to the suspension and expulsion of two students because of numerous "unexcused latenesses and absences" which constituted "disobedience or misconduct" calling for imposition of suspension or expulsion under a statute pertaining to the compulsory attendance requirement.

The case was complicated by the fact that the plaintiff students were over the compulsory-attendance age limit. Although they were permitted to attend school, they were not required to do so. Because of this fact they argued that they could not be suspended or expelled like pupils who fell within the compulsory attendance limits.

The Court of Common Pleas rejected the argument and validated the expulsions. The Commonwealth Court affirmed the ruling and emphasized that the plaintiff students did not have

> the right at their whim and caprice to pick and choose the dates when they desire to attend or the times of their arrival and departure.
> Carrying plaintiffs' arguments, in the overage situation, to their logical conclusion would present an absurd situation. Plaintiffs contend that [sections of the statute] do not apply to the overage student. Hence the board would be powerless to take any meaningful steps whatsoever to punish or deal with such conduct by the over aged. It is beyond belief that the Legislature intended such a ludicrous posture (*Id.* at 104-05).

(9) *New Rider v. Board of Educ. of Independent School Dist. No. 1, Okla.,* 480 F.2d 693 (10th Cir. 1973).

Although suspensions for violations of hair regulations have been litigated — almost to the state of boredom — one more case on the issue is referred to here because of unusual circumstances.

Three Pawnee Indian junior high school students were indefinitely suspended for their refusal to comply with a school dress code regulation stipulating the hair style for boys. The plaintiff students wore their hair in long braids because of a traditional pride in their heritage. They contended that to the Pawnee it had a "religious significance."

The United States Court of Appeals expressed the opinion that it would not interfere with the school board's action, and that plaintiffs should seek remedy in state courts:

> We believe that we would create a veritable quagmire for school boards, administrators, and teacher personnel, to attempt to wade through in their promulgation and enforcement of dress-hair codes which they may deem necessary to accomplish the objectives we have previously referred to, were we to hold that the subject dress-hair regulation implicates basic constitutional values. . . . The central core or theme is one of personal sincerity and belief. We shall not assume the responsibility of undermining the operations of the public school system by the various states through their duly chosen school authorities on such tenuous grounds. The judiciary is not designed to operate and manage school systems (*Id.* at 700).

(10) *Sapp v. Renfroe,* 372 F. Supp. 1193 (N.D. Ga. 1974).

A United States District Court upheld a school board's suspension of a high school student who refused to participate in ROTC because of his personal belief of repugnance to killing. "[H]is objection was based on religious training and his convictions were of a religious nature" (*Id.* at 1195).

The Court concluded that:

> Because Tim Sapp's objections to ROTC are based on a personal belief of repugnance to killing, and not a religious belief, the Court finds there is no objective evidence to support a finding that the Decatur High School's ROTC requirement impinged on his constitutional right to free exercise of his religion. Accordingly, the Court rules for the defendants.
>
> Although not necessary to this decision, the court notes that the record does not support a finding that Decatur High School's compulsory ROTC program is required by a compelling state interest but that the program serves a valid educational purpose and bears a rational connection to the fulfillment of the state school system's position of parens patriae by teaching students discipline, leadership, personal hygiene and first aid. The additional topics of military sciences, military organization, firearms safety and marksmanship also serve valid educational goals and do not violate Sapp's First Amendment freedom (*Id.* at 1196).

(11) *Greene v. Moore,* 373 F. Supp. 1194 (N.D. Tex. 1974).

A school board was upheld by a United States District Court in the suspension of a student who forced a confrontation with a band instructor. Evidence indicated that, without any apparent provocation or physical violence on the part of the instructor, the student threw a cup of coffee on the instructor's shirt and then "chunked" the coffee cup toward him "which resulted in minor injuries and broke his glasses" (*Id.* at 1196).

The principal called the mother of the student, advising her of the incident which resulted in suspension. At a hearing the next day, which was attended by the mother and plaintiff's attorney, it was decided to suspend the student for the remainder of the term. As pointed out by the court, the suspended student "had sufficient credits at mid-term to graduate and his suspension will not affect his right to a high school diploma" (*Id.* at 1197).

Despite certain technical deficiencies in the hearing, the court felt that it satisfied the Fourteenth Amendment requirement, and therefore concluded that:

> There is more than sufficient evidence in this record to prove that the conduct by Robert Greene on this occasion was incorrigible, and the Board was fully supported by the evidence in reaching its decision. Such evidence being before the Board, there is no denial of due process in this respect (*Id.* at 1198).

(12) *Fortman v. Texarkana School Dist. No. 7,* 514 S.W.2d 720 (Ark. 1974).

Despite the reluctance of school officials to impose, and judges to approve, *expulsion* as a disciplinary measure, there are instances in which pupils' misconduct or disobedience is of such a grave nature that their presence is so disruptive and dangerous to the

school, and detrimental to the morale of the student
body, that *expulsion* would likely be judicially condoned.

A good illustration of this legal principle is provided
by the Arkansas case where a school board suspended,
and later expelled, two tenth-grade high school girls
who deliberately planned and attacked a fellow pupil
following a verbal controversy at a dance attended by
the students. The girl victim of the attack "was kicked,
beaten, and stabbed twice in the head with a six-inch
pair of scissors. Her injuries were serious but not fatal"
(*Id.* at 721).

Counsel for the appellants argued that the board
could not legally expel a student "beyond the current
term" as stipulated in an Arkansas statute. The Circuit
Court, however, refused to accept such a narrow
interpretation of the statute, and the Supreme Court
affirmed the lower court's ruling for the expulsion, with
the following supportive statement:

> ... school directors are authorized, not only to
> exercise the powers that are expressly granted
> by statute, but also such powers as may be
> fairly implied therefrom, and from the duties
> which are expressly imposed upon them. Such
> powers will be implied when the exercise
> thereof is clearly necessary to enable them to
> carry out and perform the duties legally
> imposed upon them. ... Our school laws
> unquestionably impose upon school boards the
> duty of providing orderly educational
> institutions. Scant imagination is required to
> think of innumerable situations in which the
> power of expulsion might be the school board's
> only effective means of protecting the student

body from the disruptive, violent, or criminal actions of an incorrigibly intractable pupil (*Id.* at 722).

(13) *Ector County Independent School Dist. v. Hopkins,* 518 S.W.2d 576 (Tex. Civ. App. 1975).

A senior high school girl with a superior scholastic record acknowledged drinking wine at home during her lunch hour, knowing it was in violation of school rules. As a result she was given a one-day suspension which did not, by itself, require due process proceedings.

The one-day suspension would likely not have motivated litigation, but a more serious result did, which brought the due process question into focus. The girl was expelled from a National Honor Society and another local student group organized to foster good school spirit.

The trial court entered a permanent injunction just before the girl's graduation, ordering that she be reinstated in the two organizations. The Court of Appeals, however, held that due process had been denied and "reluctantly" ruled that judgment of the trial court would have to be remanded, stating that:

> We conclude that the one-day suspension required no more than the oral notice from the Assistant Principal concerning the alleged improper conduct upon the part of the student, and his determination at an informal hearing that she had in fact violated the school rules. We perceive the permanent expulsion from the two organizations, in which membership apparently resulted from several years of diligent efforts upon the part of Karen, both

in and out of the classroom, to be of a more serious nature in which due process was initially denied. While permanent expulsion for one violation of the organizational rules might be a greater penalty than either the trial Court or this Court would impose, we recognize quite clearly that the ultimate decision must necessarily rest with the school authorities and the faculty sponsors charged with enforcing the rules and teaching disciplinary lessons to students in the organization (*Id.* at 582).

§ 5.5. Recent decisions nullifying suspension or expulsion.

In this section reference is made to the most illustrative and recent court decisions nullifying school board attempts to discipline students by means of suspension and expulsion. The two most significant cases on this issue where the United States Supreme Court has held for the students are referred to in separate sections of this chapter.

(1) *Graham v. Knutzen,* 351 F. Supp. 642 (D. Neb. 1972).

Statutes, as well as courts, have often disagreed as to how long a student may be suspended without prior notice or hearing. In the instant case, students were suspended for what was intended to be a short period of time, but because of dissident parents in cooperation with school officials, the suspension turned out to be relatively long. Consequently, in a class action, it was charged that lack of procedural safeguards violated the due-process clause.

After considering the complicated facts of the case, it was held by the court that:

> Regardless of recalcitrance of parents and child in administrative efforts to work out improvement of student conduct by conferences, the removed child and his custodians should have had an answer from the school defining his expulsion, the reasons therefor, and such procedures, if any, to be complied with before reinstatement is allowed; and this definite responsibility must be stated in writing to those school officials to whom the power is granted (*Id.* at 644-45).

The court realized that much time was required to achieve an analysis of the educational welfare and proper placement of students in a proper educative environment, but concluded:

> *However, two or three months is unreasonable and excessive and constitutes constructive expulsion even though no formal expulsion has been decreed.* This time element must be greatly lessened by appropriate directions. Thus, if the reason for the delay is occasioned by the refusal to cooperate on the part of the student and the parent or guardian, then a definite time and adequate notice of hearing setting out the reasons for the student's removal therefrom, must be timely sent to the student and parent, together with any recommendation and terms for reinstatement which should be spelled out in such a notice (*Id.* at 667).

(2) *Cook v. Edwards,* 341 F. Supp. 307 (D.N.H. 1972).
School officials usually impose severe penalties on
students who show signs of intoxication. Such was true
in the instant case, where a fifteen-year-old female
student admittedly appeared at school in an intoxicated
condition. Therefore, the Superintendent of Schools
immediately called the girl's parents, after which he
met with them and advised them that "their daughter
had committed a serious offense," and was accordingly
being suspended, and that he was recommending to the
board that she be dismissed from the school.

The parents attended a board meeting to discuss the
matter. Whether or not there had been a *proper* meeting
was questionable. Even the judge stated: "I can now say
that it is probable that there has been a violation of
procedural due process rights," but made the following
remarks on the basis of substantive due process:

> However, the punishment of indefinite
> expulsion raises a serious question as to
> substantive due process. The result of
> indefinite expulsion may be the end of the
> plaintiff's scholastic career either because of
> its long continuance or because the plaintiff
> herself will decide to end the uncertainty of
> punishment by quitting school entirely. ... I
> can see good and sufficient reasons why a
> pupil who appears drunk on the school
> premises should be expelled from school for a
> definite period of time, or even permanently,
> if the circumstances warrant it, but I perceive
> no valid reason for making the expulsion
> indefinite. ... My concern is the plaintiff's
> constitutional rights. If judges, and
> particularly federal judges, were to tailor their

decisions as to what they thought the public wanted, the rule of law and the protection that the Constitution affords every citizen of this country would soon vanish (*Id.* at 311).

(3) *Perry v. Grenada Municipal Separate School Dist.,* 300 F. Supp. 748 (N.D. Miss. 1969).

With the increasing number of pregnancies in high schools, the attendance status of unwed mothers has become a litigious issue. In this first applicable case brought before a federal court, it was revealed that the Grenada, Mississippi School had denied readmission to two young unwed mothers.

As a consequence, the girls brought action against the school board with the claim that the exclusion policy of the board violated the due process and equal protection clauses of the Fourteenth Amendment. The court agreed with the girls' complaint, and stated that:

> Unwed mothers could not be excluded from high schools of the district for sole reason that they were unwed mothers . . . unless on a fair hearing before the school authorities they were found to be so lacking in moral character that their presence in the school would taint the education of other students (*Id.* at 748-49).

Apparently the judicial view was that an unwed mother should have the opportunity for rehabilitation and to continue an education for the welfare of the individual as well as society. The court stressed the fact that "a girl has one child out of wedlock does not forever brand her as a scarlet woman undeserving of any chance for rehabilitation or the opportunity for future education . . ." (*Id.* 753).

(4) *Ordway v. Hargraves,* 323 F. Supp. 1155 (D. Mass. 1971).

The attendance status of an unwed pregnant student was litigated in a 1971 case in Massachusetts before a United States District Court. Here the high school principal attempted to carry out a board policy which stipulated that: "Whenever an unmarried girl enrolled in North Middlesex Regional High School shall be known to be pregnant, her membership in the school shall be immediately terminated" (*Id.* at 1156).

School officials contended that since the age group of students in the school (twelve to fourteen) was "still flexible in their attitudes; they might be led to believe that the school authorities are condoning premarital relations if they were to allow girl students in plaintiff's situation to remain in school" (*Id.* at 1158).

When the pregnancy of the girl was detected, she was informed that she could no longer attend *regular* classes, although she could make use of certain school facilities after formal dismissal time.

After considering testimony as to the girl's physical and mental condition and the unharmful effect of her presence in the classroom, the court ordered that she be reinstated to her classes. The rationale for the court's decision follows:

> In summary, no danger to petitioner's physical or mental health resultant from her attending classes during regular school hours has been shown; no likelihood that her presence will cause any disruption of or

interference with school activities or pose a
threat of harm to others has been shown; and
no valid educational or other reason to justify
her segregation and to require her to receive
a type of educational treatment which is not
the equal of that given to all others in her class
has been shown (*Id.* at 1158).

(5) *Houston v. Prosser,* 361 F. Supp. 295 (N.D. Ga.
1973).

Another case involving the issue of an unmarried
mother's right to attend school arose in Georgia, where
a 15-year-old girl challenged a school policy denying her
readmission to school as a regular daytime student. The
policy reads as follows:

Any person who marries or is found to have
become a parent during the course of his or her
public education in the City of Decatur shall
not be permitted to continue his or her
education in said Decatur School System as a
regular daytime student ... (*Id.* at 296).
Students coming within the scope of this rule
shall be entitled to participate in a fully
accredited educational program to be taught at
night ... (*Id.* at 297).

Significantly, tuition and textbooks were provided
without charge to daytime students but not to night
students.

After the facts of the case were heard, the court held
that the school officials' policy of excluding plaintiff
from regular daytime classes did not penalize her
fundamental right of procreation. But the court also
held that the policy of requiring plaintiff to pay tuition

and provide for textbooks to attend night school denied equal protection.

> Therefore the court finds that defendants' policy, although fair on its face, denies plaintiff the equal protection of the laws as it is applied (*Id.* at 299).

(6) *Goetz v. Ansell,* 477 F.2d 636 (2d Cir. 1973).

A United States District Court dismissed a petition to enjoin school board officials from disciplining a student for remaining seated during the flag-pledge ceremony. On appeal, however, the United States Court of Appeals, Second Circuit, reversed the ruling of the lower court.

The plaintiff Goetz, who was a senior, an honor student, and president of his class, refused "to participate in the Pledge of Allegiance because he believes that there [isn't] liberty and justice for all in the United States" (*Id.* at 636).

Following his refusal to participate, he was offered the option of either leaving the room or standing silently during the pledge ceremony. He declined the option, even though in adhering to that position, he was faced with suspension from school.

The court admitted that a student's conduct that materially disrupts classwork or involves substantial disorder or invasion of the rights of others is subject to disciplining. But it held in this case that the facts did not justify the application of discipline. "There is no evidence here of disruption of classwork or disorder or invasion of the rights of others. The record is just to the contrary . . ." (*Id.* at 638).

In conclusion the court stated:

> While we do not share plaintiff's resistance
> to pledging allegiance to this nation, his
> reservations of belief must be protected. In
> time, perhaps, he will recognize that such
> protection is sound ground for a firmer trust
> in his country (*Id.* at 638-39).

(7) *Smith v. Miller,* 514 P.2d 377 (Kan. 1973).

Gary Smith, a student, was *expelled* from school by
the board of education for repeated assaults on other
students. He had previously been suspended several
times for assaults.

A district court upheld the expulsion and the student
appealed to the Supreme Court of Kansas, which
reversed the ruling of the lower court because of
defects in the expulsion procedure. The Supreme Court
agreed with Smith, who claimed he was deprived of
procedural due process because he was denied "the
right of confrontation and cross-examination of the
witness against him."

The Supreme Court's rationale for its decision is
somewhat evasive as indicated by the following
passage:

> Courts which have considered the issue of
> the student's right to cross-examination of the
> witnesses against him have divided in different
> directions, indicating the difficulty of
> prescribing any hard and fast rule applicable
> to all situations. It would appear at the present
> time that a majority of jurisdictions favors
> granting the right under situations similar to
> that present here. We will attempt no analysis

of the many decisions other than to say that in
some cases it appears no question has been
raised where the right has been exercised, in
some it has been either unqualifiedly granted
or denied and in others either qualifiedly
granted or refused. Although a federal
constitutional right is involved the United
States Supreme Court has not spoken directly
on the issue ... (*Id.* at 386).

(8) *Graber v. Kniola,* 52 Mich. App. 269, 216 N.W.2d
925 (1974).

The litigious issue of dress codes has been grossly
overstressed. This case, however, is referred to because
of its recency, and, hopefully, its conclusiveness. The
case grew out of an action by students challenging the
validity of a provision of the school dress code which
stipulated the required length of hair for male students.

A Circuit Court upheld the validity of the provision,
whereupon the students appealed. The Court of Appeals
of Michigan reversed the decision of the lower court.
However, its reluctance to delve very deeply into the
issue is indicated by the following remarks:

There is really very little point to an erudite
and extended discussion about the right of
school authorities to prescribe reasonable
regulations of personal appearance for school
attendance during school hours.
Nor will it benefit bench, bar, or school
authorities to hold forth at length on the
undoubted right of students to choose
individual attire in their hair styling.
Obviously, this is not to say that young ladies
of varying degrees of comeliness may

(Michigan weather permitting) attend classes in bikinis. Nor may male students emulate Tarzan and attend classes in loin-cloths. Mr. Justice Cardoza, of revered memory, once cogently observed, in substance, that the law is a matter of degree (*Id.* at 926).

The court stated in conclusion:

Despite our disagreement with the conclusion of the learned trial judge in this case, we do wish to commend him for his extremely well documented opinion, contra to ours (*Id.* at 927).

(9) *St. Ann v. Palisi*, 495 F.2d 423 (5th Cir. 1974). This case grew out of an unusual school board regulation which authorized school officials to suspend pupils from school for the misconduct of their parents. The misconduct here was a mother's action in striking an assistant school principal "on the face with her fist in which she was holding a key chain."

The mother brought action under the Civil Rights Act for injunctive relief claiming her children's constitutional rights had been infringed and that the school board regulation authorizing suspension was invalid.

A United States District Court dismissed the complaint, and the mother appealed to the Court of Appeals where it was "held that the regulation was invalid as infringing the constitutional principle that one may be punished only on the basis of his personal guilt" (*Id.* at 423).

The Court of Appeals made the following pertinent statement to support its stand:

> As the district court indicated, school principals must be given considerable freedom to achieve effective school administration, but courts should not hesitate to act when fundamental constitutional liberties are contravened. Freedom from punishment in the absence of *personal* guilt is a fundamental concept in the American scheme of justice. In order to intrude upon this fundamental liberty, governments must satisfy a substantial burden of justification. Since the school officials have failed to meet this burden we must vacate the district court's order of dismissal with prejudice with respect to the claims of the minor plaintiffs, and remand for proceedings consistent with this opinion (*Id.* at 425).

(10) *"M. W." v. Bd. of Educ. of the Freehold Regional High School Dist., Monmouth County.* Decision of the Commissioner of Education of New Jersey, February 26, 1975.

M. W., a minor enrolled in the eleventh grade, was expelled as a result of his alleged involvement in an assault upon another pupil. M. W. insisted his expulsion was illegal, whereas the Board denied any improper or illegal act.

Apparently there was much conflicting testimony by the various witnesses at the expulsion hearing. Moreover, there was considerable doubt as to the legality of the Board's action by the hearing examiner who "concludes that the vote taken in caucus session

was not a legal act of the Board. There is in the entire
record no evidence that at any time a motion was made
and seconded in a public meeting of the Board and
passed by a majority of the members present to expel
the two pupils" (*Id.* at 8). He then "recommended that
the Commissioner determine that M. W. was not legally
expelled." The Commissioner "accepts the findings of
the hearing examiner and holds them for his own" (*Id.*
at 11).

> The Commissioner is constrained to
> comment that holding expulsion hearings as
> closed sessions of boards of education is in the
> best interests of minor pupils and their parents
> and families in that it preserves their right of
> privacy. It is also in the best interests of
> maintaining an orderly proceeding. Likewise,
> a board may consider its findings in caucus
> sessions. It is not proper, however, to reach a
> final determination by voting to expel or not
> to expel while in caucus session. To do so
> reduces to a sham the official legal action of
> a board which must be taken in public session
> as required by N. J. S. A. 18A:10-6 (*Id.* at
> 12-13).

§ 5.6. A landmark decision (Goss v. Lopez) regarding adequacy of procedural due process.

Anyone who follows the news media is aware of the
landmark decision of the United States Supreme Court
in *Goss v. Lopez*, 95 S. Ct. 729 (Ohio 1975), holding that
students suspended for short periods of time were
nevertheless entitled to minimal due process under the
Fourteenth Amendment. In essence, the ruling struck

down an Ohio law which authorized school officials to suspend a student for ten days or less without giving the student advance notice of the charges against him and without affording him the opportunity to defend himself.

The case report fails to describe in detail just what the charges against the students were which prompted the litigated suspensions. But apparently the suspension in question arose out of a period of widespread student unrest in the Columbus Public Schools in 1971. Some students were suspended on account of disruptive or disobedient conduct in the presence of the school administrator who ordered the suspensions. One student was alleged to have even physically attacked a police officer who was attempting to remove a disruptive student from the school auditorium.

Dwight Lopez, whose name appears in the title of the case, was suspended for allegedly causing a disturbance in the lunchroom, which involved some physical damage to school property. Lopez, however, testified "that he was not a party to the destructive conduct but was instead an innocent bystander. . . . there is no evidence in the record indicating the official basis for concluding otherwise. Lopez never had a hearing" (*Id.* at 734).

On the basis of evidence, a three-judge court declared the plaintiff students were denied due process of law because they were suspended without a hearing prior to the suspension or within a reasonable time thereafter. The lower court ruled that the regulations to the contrary in the Ohio Rev. Code "were unconstitutional in permitting such suspension." Moreover, it was ordered that "all references to plaintiffs' suspensions be removed from school files" (*Id.* at 734). The United States Supreme Court *affirmed* the ruling of the United States District Court for the Southern District of Ohio.

Mr. Justice White, who wrote for the majority, described what it considered a proper hearing in a suspension case in the following terms:

> The difficulty is that our schools are vast and complex. Some modicum of discipline and order is essential if the educational function is to be performed. Events calling for discipline are frequent occurrences and sometimes require immediate, effective action. Suspension is considered not only to be a necessary tool to maintain order but a valuable educational device. The prospect of imposing elaborate hearing requirements in every suspension case is viewed with great concern, and many school authorities may well prefer the untrammeled power to act unilaterally, unhampered by rules about notice and hearing. But it would be a strange disciplinary system in an educational institution if no communication was sought by the disciplinarian with the student in an effort to inform him of his defalcation and to let him tell his side of the story in order to make sure that an injustice is not done . . . (*Id.* at 739).
>
> We do not believe that school authorities must be totally free from notice and hearing requirements if their schools are to operate

with acceptable efficiency. Students facing temporary suspension have interests qualifying for protection of the Due Process Clause, and due process requires, in connection with a suspension of 10 days or less, that the student be given oral or written notice of the charges against him and, if he denies them, an explanation of the evidence the authorities have and an opportunity to present his side of the story. The clause requires at least these rudimentary precautions against unfair or mistaken findings of misconduct and arbitrary exclusion from school (*Id.* at 739-40).

In conclusion, the court made it clear that the decision rendered in the instant case would not necessarily apply to other cases in different circumstances:

We should also make it clear that we have addressed ourselves solely to the short suspension, not exceeding 10 days. Longer suspension or expulsions for the remainder of the school term, or permanently, may require more formal procedures. Nor do we put aside the possibility that in unusual situations, although involving only a short suspension, something more than the rudimentary procedure will be required (*Id.* at 741).

Because of the split 5-4 decision, it is logical to assume there were strong arguments in the minority opinion written by Justice Powell who was joined by the Chief Justice and Justices Blackmun and Rehnquist. The logic of the minority follows:

The Court today invalidates an Ohio statute that permits student suspensions from school without a hearing "for not more than ten days." The decision unnecessarily opens avenues for judicial intervention in the operation of our public schools that may affect adversely the quality of education. The Court holds for the first time that the federal courts, rather than educational officials and state legislatures, have the authority to determine the rules applicable to routine classroom discipline of children and teenagers in the public schools. It justifies this unprecedented intrusion into the process of elementary and secondary education by identifying a new constitutional right: the right of a student not to be suspended for as much as a single day without notice and a due process hearing either before or promptly following the suspension (*Id.* at 741).

One of the more disturbing aspects of today's decision is its indiscriminate reliance upon the judiciary, and the adversary process as the means of resolving many of the most routine problems arising in the classroom. In mandating due process procedures the Court misapprehends the reality of the normal teacher-pupil relationships (*Id.* at 746).

If, as seems apparent, the Court will now require due process procedures whenever such routine school decisions are challenged, the impact upon public education will be serious indeed. The discretion and judgment of federal courts across the land often will be substituted for that of the 50-state legislatures, the 14,000 school boards and the 2,000,000 teachers who heretofore have been responsible for the administration of the American public school system. If the Court perceives a rational and analytically sound distinction between the discretionary decision by school authorities to suspend a pupil for a brief period, and the types of discretionary school decisions described above, it would be prudent to articulate it in today's opinion. Otherwise, the federal courts should prepare themselves for a vast new role in society (*Id.* at 748-49).

§ 5.7. A startling decision (Wood v. Strickland) involving liability of school board members.

What originally started out as a "prank" developed into a case (*Wood v. Strickland,* 95 S. Ct. 992 (Ark. 1975)) which ran the gamut of the federal courts. The relevant facts of the case reveal that two sixteen-year-old girls in the tenth grade decided to "spike" the punch which was intended to be served at the meeting of an extracurricular school organization attended by parents and students. The girls experienced second thoughts about the wisdom of their prank, but at the urging of fellow pupils, went through with it. The punch was served at the meeting without apparent effect, which is understandable since testimony at the trial put the alcohol content of the punch served at only "0.91 per cent." Nevertheless the students were expelled for violating a school regulation, whereupon they sought damages and injunctive relief from a district court.

The District Court held for the school board on the ground that "they were immune from damage suits absent proof of malice in the sense of ill will toward

respondents." The girls appealed to the Eighth Circuit
Court of Appeals, where it was held that the facts
showed a violation of *substantive due process*. Then it
was finally carried to the United States Supreme Court
where it was held that (1) the girls had not been
afforded due process of law and (2) school board
members, as individuals, are not immune from liability
for compensating damages under the Civil Rights Act
of 1871, which, in essence, provides:

> Every person who under cover of any
> statute, ordinance, regulation, custom, or
> usage of any State, subjects or causes to be
> subjected any citizen of the U. S. . . . to
> deprivation of any rights, privileges and
> immunities secured by the Constitution and
> laws, shall be liable to the party injured in an
> action at law, suit in equity or other proper
> proceedings for redress."

With respect to the pertinent issue of absolute
immunity of individual school board members, the court
responded:

> [A]bsolute immunity would not be justified
> since it would not sufficiently increase the
> ability of school officials to exercise their
> discretion in a forthright manner to warrant
> the absence of a remedy for students subjected
> to intentional or otherwise inexcusable
> deprivations (*Id.* at 1000).

The thrust of the High Court's opinion regarding the
issue whether immunity from money damages would be

granted is contained in the following lengthy paragraph
— without embellishment from this author:

> The disagreement between the Court of
> Appeals and the District Court over the
> immunity standard in this case has been put in
> terms of an "objective" versus a "subjective"
> test of good faith. As we see it, the appropriate
> standard necessarily contains elements of
> both. The official must himself be acting
> sincerely and with a belief that he is doing
> right, but an act violating a student's
> constitutional rights can be no more justified
> by ignorance or disregard of settled,
> indisputable law on the part of one entrusted
> with supervision of students' daily lives than
> by the presence of actual malice. To be entitled
> to a special exemption from the categorical
> remedial language of § 1983 in a case in which
> his action violated a student's constitutional
> rights, a school board member, who has
> voluntarily undertaken the task of supervising
> the operation of the school and the activities of
> the students, must be held to a standard of
> conduct based not only on permissible
> intentions, but also on knowledge of the basic,
> unquestioned constitutional rights of his
> charges. Such a standard neither imposes an
> unfair burden upon a person assuming a
> responsible public office requiring a high
> degree of intelligence and judgment for the
> proper fulfillment of its duties, nor an
> unwarranted burden in light of the value which
> civil rights have in our legal system. Any lesser
> standard would deny much of the promise of
> § 1983. Therefore, in the specific context of
> school discipline, we hold that a school board

member is not immune from liability for damages under § 1983 if he knew or reasonably should have known that the action he took within his sphere of official responsibility would violate the constitutional rights of the student affected, or if he took the action with the malicious intention to cause a deprivation of constitutional rights or other injury to the student. That is not to say that school board members are "charged with predicting the future course of constitutional law." . . . A compensatory award will be appropriate only if the school board member has acted with such an impermissible motivation or with such disregard of the student's clearly established constitutional rights that his action cannot reasonably be characterized as being in good faith (*Id.* at 1000-01).

This case, like *Goss v. Lopez*, resulted in another split 5-4 decision with the same line-up for the majority and minority opinions. Justice White, who wrote the *majority* opinion, was joined by Justices Douglas, Brennan, Stewart and Marshall; whereas Justice Powell, who wrote the *dissenting* opinion, was joined by Chief Justice Burger, and Justices Blackmun and Rehnquist.

Aside from the constitutional questions of the majority opinion, the four dissenting judges expressed their concern in the following two excerpts about the injurious effects the decision might have upon the future recruitment of school board members:

. . . The Court's decision appears to rest on an unwarranted assumption as to what lay

officials know or can know about the law and
constitutional rights. These officials will now
act at the peril of some judge or jury
subsequently finding that a good-faith belief
as to the applicable law was mistaken and
hence actionable (*Id.* at 1004).

There are some 20,000 school boards, each
with five or more members, and thousands of
school superintendents and school principals.
Most of the school board members are
popularly elected, drawn from the citizenry at
large, and possess no unique competency in
divining the law. Few cities and counties
provide any compensation for service on school
boards, and often it is difficult to persuade
qualified persons to assume the burdens of this
important function in our society. Moreover,
even if counsel's advice constitutes a defense,
it may safely be assumed that few school
boards and school officials have ready access
to counsel or indeed have deemed it necessary
to consult counsel on the countless decisions
that necessarily must be made in the operation
of our public schools (*Id.* at 1005).

§ 5.8. Necessity for suitable alternatives to exclusion.

The behavior of some students is so disruptive and
dangerous that school boards are legally justified in
separating them from other students by expulsion or
long-term suspension. Such drastic action, however,
carries with it a responsibility to ensure appropriate
educational alternatives.

The judiciary is well aware of this fact as frequently
found in court opinions upholding expulsion, qualified

with the recommendation that efforts be made to find
suitable alternatives for regular school attendance. A
statement in the opinion of a federal court (*Lee v. Mason
County Bd. of Educ.*, 490 F.2d 458 (5th Cir. 1974)) is
illustrative:

> We do not minimize the children's
> misbehavior. They are undisciplined, defiant,
> and abusive, and their mother was
> uncooperative with school officials in
> attempting to deal with them. Nor are we
> insensitive to the difficulties faced by school
> officials in attempting to curb disorderly
> interferences with the primary task of the
> school, which is education. But a sentence of
> banishment from the educational system is,
> insofar as the institution has power to act, the
> extreme penalty, the ultimate punishment. In
> our increasingly technological society getting
> at least a high school education is almost
> necessary for survival. Stripping a child of
> access to educational opportunity is a life
> sentence to second-rate citizenship, unless the
> child has the financial ability to migrate to
> another school system or enter private school
> (*Id.* at 460).

The New Jersey Commissioner of Education has
ruled upon numerous cases involving expulsions and
long-term suspensions, in which he frequently mentions
the school board's responsibility to see that the
excluded student is not deprived of further educational
opportunity. A well-stated example is found in the case

of *"R. K." v. Board of Educ. of the Township of Lakewood*, (1973) in which the Commissioner stated:

> . . . Termination of a pupil's right to attend the public schools of a district is a drastic and desperate remedy which should be employed only when no other course is possible. . . . It is obvious that a board of education cannot wash its hands of a problem by recourse to expulsion. While such an act may resolve an immediate problem for the school, it may likewise create a host of others involving not only the pupil but the community and society at large. The Commissioner suggests, therefore, that boards of education who are forced to take expulsion action cannot shrug off responsibility but should make every effort to see that the child comes under the aegis of another agency able to deal with the problem. The Commissioner urges boards of education, therefore, to recognize expulsion as a negative and defeatist kind of last-ditch expedient resorted to only after and based upon competent professional evaluation and recommendation.

The New Jersey Commissioner of Education also ruled in the case of *Wharton v. Board of Educ. of the City of Bridgeton*, Decision of the New Jersey Commissioner of Education (1972) that "since expulsion of a pupil is an extremely drastic action, a board of education is required to provide an offer of alternate instruction, either in an evening school or at home, for either a regular or an equivalency diploma."

In a *Report by the Children's Defense Fund of the Washington Research Project, Inc.*, "Children Out of School in America" (1974), further expression is given to the potentially harmful results accruing from any exclusion from a regular school. Under the caption "What It Means to a Child to be Suspended," the *Report* states:

> While precise measurement of the psychological and educational harm done by a suspension is impossible, it is clear that any exclusion from school interrupts the child's educational process and forcibly removes the child from his normal daily environment. It is not clear what good such punishment does. In fact, it may work against the child's improvement in at least four ways. First, it forbids the child from participating in academic work. If children with discipline problems also are weak in their studies, their missed classes, assignments and exams may doom them to fail completely. Second, suspensions merely remove troubling children. They do not set in motion diagnostic or supportive services that might uncover and remediate the causes of a child's behavior. Thus, suspensions deny help to children. Third, suspension is a powerful label that not only stigmatizes a child while in school (or out of it), but follows the child beyond school to later academic or employment pursuits. And fourth, suspensions are highly correlated with juvenile delinquency. Putting children out of school, leaving them idle with no supervision, especially when they are demonstrating they have problems, leaves children alone to cope with their future (p. 135).

Chapter 6

UNORTHODOX PRACTICES OF DISCIPLINING

§ 6.1. Exclusion from graduation exercises and denial of diploma.
§ 6.2. Reduction of grades as a punitive measure.
§ 6.3. Humiliation of students before classmates.
§ 6.4. Deprivation of privileges for married students.
§ 6.5. Deprivation of privileges for members of secret societies.

§ 6.1. Exclusion from graduation exercises and denial of diploma.

(1) *Valentine v. Independent School Dist. of Casey,* 191 Iowa 1100, 183 N.W. 434 (1921).

This is the first reported case involving exclusion from graduation ceremonies for infraction of school-board directives. The case report is not without its elements of humor.

Apparently last-minute directions from the school board stipulated that "caps and gowns should be worn on that auspicious occasion, and the same were furnished by the board." Three of six girls who were to have graduated refused to wear the caps which were misfits and the gowns because of the offensive odor emanating from recent fumigation with formaldehyde. Consequently the defiant girls "were not permitted to occupy seats on the platform and to whom diplomas were not granted" (*Id.* at 435).

From evidence brought before the Supreme Court of Iowa, it was revealed that the plaintiff in the case, one of the girls excluded from graduation ceremonies, had achieved high academic honors. "She was an exceptionally strong student, and was the valedictorian of her class."

In holding for the plaintiff, the court stated:

> ... The issuance of a diploma by the school
> board to a pupil who satisfactorily completes
> the prescribed course of study and who is
> otherwise qualified is mandatory, and,
> although such duty is not expressly enjoined
> upon the board by statute, it does arise by
> necessary and reasonable implication.
> ... This plaintiff ... having complied with
> all the rules and regulations precedent to
> graduation, may not be denied her diploma by
> the arbitrary action of the school board
> subsequent to her being made the recipient of
> the honors of graduation. It is also clear that
> plaintiff is entitled to a certificate of her
> grades (*Id.* at 437).

(2) *Ladson v. Board of Educ., Union Free School Dist.
#9,* 323 N.Y.S.2d 545 (Sup. Ct. 1971).

Just a half century later than *Valentine,* this case
grew out of an incident in which a senior black girl was
excluded from participating in the graduation
ceremonies because of an alleged assault on the high
school principal. The alleged attack took place during
a bomb threat and stonings between white and black
students.

As a consequence, among the penalties imposed the
girl was advised that "she was to receive her graduation
diploma in the principal's office ... rather than at the
regular graduation ceremony" (*Id.* at 547).

After failing to find statutory authority for school

officials to take such action, the court referred to the graduation ceremony as an affair

> at which the school authorities and the families and friends of graduates, honor the educational achievement of those who receive their diplomas. Nowhere in the statutory scheme of public school administration does there appear express authority to direct suspension from participation in those ceremonies as a disciplinary measure directed at students otherwise qualified to participate (*Id.* at 549).

In holding for the girl, the court stated its rationale in the following passage:

> The Court is persuaded that punishment and discipline should be responsive to the educational goals to which the school system is dedicated. Courts are dedicated not only to the administration of laws, but to the pursuit of justice, and the two ideals must come together. The justice of the situation favors graduation attendance. We have here a student of demonstrated dedication, who has persevered through all of her term in high school and has completed her final year under adversity, even though some of that adversity may be of her own doing. She has been accepted at college. Her graduation ceremony is important and meaningful to her personally and in her family which has never before had a high school graduate. She has no other record of school disorder than the one incident here involved. It would indeed be a distortion of our educational process in this period of youthful discontentment to snatch from a

young woman at the point of educational fruition the savoring of her educational success. The Court believes that not to be a reasonable punishment meant to encourage the best educational results (*Id.* at 550).

(3) *"K. C." v. Board of Educ. of Collingswood* (Decision of the New Jersey Commissioner of Education (June 20, 1973)).

K. C., the petitioner in this case, contends that only a grade of "F" in an art course, which was not averaged with her other grades, prevented her from having a "passing average" for graduation. Consequently, at the last hour she was denied the right to stand with her class at the ninth-grade graduation exercises and was deprived of a diploma from the junior high school.

In his decision the Commissioner pointed out that there was no irreparable harm, since the girl was admitted to the senior high school despite her lack of a certificate of admission. Even though it was too late to offer any relief with respect to the "graduation exercises," the Commissioner stated he "deplores the determination by school officials that denied petitioner the opportunity to participate in her ninth-grade graduation exercises." Therefore, he directed the Board "to issue her the same kind of diploma awarded all ninth graders who graduated."

(4) *In re O'Brien,* 13 Ed. Dept. Rep. (New York Commissioner of Education Decision No. 8828 (1974)).

According to a statement extracted from the *Nolpe School Law Reporter,* May-June 1974, p. 12:

The Commissioner ordered the board to

award petitioner's daughter a high school diploma. Held, that it is well established that a student may not be denied a high school diploma solely on the basis of failure to complete four years of physical education where a valid reason for the deficiency is demonstrated. During her sophomore year the student, who was born with a congenital spinal deformity, underwent corrective surgery which necessitated her hospitalization and confinement at home.

(5) *R. H., a minor, by his parent and guardian, ad litem v. Board of Educ. of Township of Delano* (Decision of the New Jersey Commissioner of Education, Dec. 1974).

Where a pupil was guilty of uttering an obscene expletive to a teacher during the course of a practice for eighth-grade promotion exercises, the denial to the student of the right to participate in such exercises was held to be proper and not excessive punishment.

§ 6.2. Reduction of grades as a punitive measure.

(1) *Wermuth v. Bernstein & Bd. of Educ. of the Township of Livingston, Essex County* (Decision of the New Jersey Commissioner of Education, 121 (1965)).

In this case the Commissioner cautioned that marks and grades should not be used to serve disciplinary purposes and added that

the use of marks and grades as deterrents or as punishment is likewise usually ineffective in producing the desired results and is educationally not defensible. Whatever system of *marks and grades* a school may devise will have serious inherent limitations at best, and it *must not be further handicapped by attempting to serve disciplinary purposes* also.

(2) *Minorics v. Board of Educ. of Phillipsburg* (Decision of the New Jersey Commissioner of Education, March 24, 1972).

This was a class action seeking relief from a grading policy alleged to be used as an "improper" disciplinary measure. Pertinent stipulations of the policy were as follows:

(a) Students in the Phillipsburg Schools receive zero in all subjects on those days when they are truant from school and in those instances when, because of their own actions, they are in suspension from the privilege of school attendance.

(b) Students may make up tests that they may have missed on such days. These test results are then averaged in with all other marks received during that quarter . . . including the assigned zero (p. 3).

After reviewing a number of decisions from previous cases, the Commissioner agreed:

There can be no doubt that the zero as awarded herein has the effect of a penalty that dilutes achievement, and that, in some instances where there may be few objective grades, the zero has a significant impact on the final grade that a student may earn. The zero weighs the record down (p. 9).

The Commissioner refrained from directing the Board to change the "grading policies for the present school year" but proposed "that pertinent guidelines be developed" and sent to the Commissioner "promptly following their adoption."

(3) *Dorsey v. Bale,* 521 S.W.2d 76 (Ky. Ct. of App. 1975).

This case grew out of a contested regulation in the school's handbook which provided that:

> Absences for any other reason and failure to follow the outlined procedure will constitute an unexcused absence and work will not be allowed to be made up and furthermore five (5) points will be deducted from the total nine-weeks grade for each unexcused absence from each class during the grading period (*Id.* at 77).

Bale, the appellee in this case, had his grades reduced for unexcused absences as an additional punishment leading to his suspension from classes. The Board argued that it had the statutory authority to "do all things necessary to accomplish the purpose for which it was created" and was therefore authorized to "make and adopt rules and regulations for the conduct of pupils."

That argument did not prevent a circuit court from declaring the regulation to be invalid. The Court of Appeals affirmed the ruling of the lower court, after reviewing the contested statute which specifically authorizes suspension or expulsion for gross misconduct but finding no authorization whatsoever for lowering grades as a punitive measure. In support of its decision the court remarked:

> We are of the opinion that this statute, under which Tommy Bale was suspended, clearly preempts the right of school officials to promulgate disciplinary regulations that impose additional punishment for the conduct that results in suspension. If the conduct of the student in the judgment of the school authorities warrants invoking the statutory authority to suspend, and school authorities do suspend, they have the right to determine the duration of suspension so that such action constitutes a complete punishment for the offense (*Id.* at 78).

§ 6.3. Humiliation of students before classmates.

Some teachers can concoct disciplinary policies which are more objectionable than mere corporal punishment. Humiliation of a student before his classmates can be more deleterious than the infliction of physical pain, according to an article in which the author states:

> Instead of now punishing children in private, and having the event done with, children are now branded with tumultuous criticisms from their teachers, not in private but in front of an entire class and the peers of the individual to whom this more civilized form of punishment is being inflicted. . . .
> Corporal punishment or so it is referred, was banished at least in part for fear of children being physically abused and bruised. What

about the bruises inflicted upon the mind? These bruises do not go away as quickly as those of the flesh and yet little seems to be done to prevent punishment in the form of humiliation, embarrassment, harassment and the destruction of children's self-concept at an age when it should be growing and expanding in confidence combined with a sense of personal identity (p. 213). (Mary Dianne McCarthy, "Humanitarianism and Corporal Punishment," *Education,* Vol. 95, No. 3, pp. 212-15 (Spring, 1975).

(1) *Gordon v. Oak Park School Dist. No. 97,* 24 Ill. App. 3d 131, 320 N.E.2d 389 (1974).

A verbal lashing is one disciplinary method which may not result in a teacher's being held liable. In the instant case, the court "recognized that within the broad delegation of parental authority, a teacher has the right to verbally chastise a pupil" (*Id.* at 392).

Even though the teacher intentionally "humiliated, degraded and shamed (a student) with disparaging remarks," the teacher will not be held liable without "proof of wantonness or malice." It is significant to note here that virtually every form of pupil discipline — including corporal punishment — is legally permissible with that qualification.

(2) *Celestine v. Lafayette Parish School Bd.,* 284 So. 2d 650 (La. 1973).

In this extreme case it was ruled that poor judgment, coupled with a lack of an educational purpose, was just cause for dismissal of a teacher who required pupils to write a vulgar word 1,000 times, in the presence of their classmates, as a disciplinary measure for having uttered the word.

The events leading to the litigation in this case are described as follows:

> Shortly after his class reconvened following the noon lunch period on the above mentioned date, plaintiff was confronted by several students who told him that two of his girl students had been using "bad words." Plaintiff thereupon asked the two girls in the presence of other members of the class whether they had been using vulgar language, and when they responded that they had, he instructed each of them to write the vulgar word 1,000 times and to turn that work in to the principal for his signature, and to the parents for their signatures. One of the two girls to whom the assignment was given was eleven years of age at that time.
>
> Pursuant to his instruction given to them by plaintiff, each of these girls began writing a four-lettered word, beginning with the letter "F," being an extremely vulgar word meaning sexual intercourse. They spent the rest of that day carrying out the assignment of writing that word 1,000 times . . . (*Id.* at 652).

On the following day, school officials met with the plaintiff teacher (Celestine) to discuss the incident, and later the Superintendent of Schools wrote a letter to the offending teacher advising him that he was being suspended indefinitely from duty without pay. He was then given the option of resigning or facing a recommendation of the superintendent that he be dismissed for incompetency.

The teacher refused to resign, so the board took formal action by dismissing him. When the case was heard, the court refused to interfere with the board's action.

§ 6.4. Deprivation of privileges for married students.

The concern of school officials over student marriages is reflected in the numerous punitive policies formulated to deprive married students of participation in "extracurricular activities" — particularly athletics. Some of the regulations have been so objectionable and controversial as to trigger litigation.

(1) *Kissick v. Garland Independent School Dist.,* 330 S.W.2d 708 (Tex. Ct. App. 1959).

This was the first applicable case. It received nationwide attention from students of school law and served for over a decade as a guiding principle on other cases dealing with the same issue.

The facts of the case reveal that Kissick, a football player, sought to restrain enforcement of a board resolution which provided that "married students be restricted wholly to classroom work and that they be barred from participating in athletics." Among the contentions made by Kissick was that (1) the resolution in question was arbitrary, discriminatory and unreasonable, and (2) it was violative of public policy in that it penalized marriage.

It was "admitted that physical education is a required course of the school; the playing of football being sufficient to obtain credit for that compulsory course;

also that the resolution was passed, in the main, to discourage juvenile marriages among students . . ." (*Id.* at 709-10).

Nevertheless, the Texas court upheld the board regulation. Apparently the court placed considerable weight upon the findings of a PTA study indicating "ill effects of married students participating in extra-curricular activities with unmarried students."

(2) *Cochrane v. Board of Educ. of Mesick Consolidated School Dist.,* 360 Mich. 390, 103 N.W.2d 569 (1960).

The year after *Kissick* another case originated in Michigan concerning the marriage issue. Two boys involved in the case were married several weeks before the school board adopted a rule that "Married students attending school shall not be eligible to participate in any co-curricular activities — such as competitive sports." The two boys, who had previously participated in competitive sports, filed a writ of mandamus to compel the school board to admit them to the co-curricular activities.

After a lower court ruled that the board resolution was legal, the case was appealed to the state supreme court, but before it could be heard there, the two boys graduated, thereby making the issue "moot." Nevertheless, the higher court rendered an "advisory opinion." The court was evenly divided on reversing and affirming the ruling of the lower court. Some school-law authorities believed this portended an eventual reversal of the precedent set by the *Kissick* decision.

(3) *State v. Stevenson,* 27 Ohio App. 2d 223, 189 N.E.2d 181 (1962).

This case resulted from a board regulation which retroactively prohibited a married boy who was a "star" basketball player from continuing to participate in the school's athletic program. In upholding the board regulation, the court was apparently influenced by a statistical report showing an "alarming" marriage-dropout relationship. The court ignored an opinion of the Attorney General of Ohio who contended that "a board of education may not lawfully adopt a regulation prohibiting married students from participating in extra-curricular activities promoted by the school as part of the regular school program. He made the observation that extra-curricular activities 'have become an integral part of contemporary education'" (*Id.* at 187).

The court reasoned that the boy's "responsibility as a father and concern therefor might adversely affect his performance on the court; other things might occur in connection with his playing basketball which could easily affect, even destroy, his future as a college player, thus preventing his receipt of an athletic scholarship" (*Id.* at 187).

(4) *Starkey v. Board of Educ. of Davis County School Dist.,* 14 Utah 2d 227, 381 P.2d 718 (1963).

The fourth case to reach a state supreme court arose in Utah in 1963. The factors involved in the case were quite similar to those in the three preceding cases reported. The court's ruling was also similar to those in the other jurisdictions in that the board's regulation prohibiting a married boy from participating in the athletic program was upheld. As did the other courts, the Utah Supreme Court emphasized the fact that school boards, and not the courts, are endowed with the power to regulate the schools. Judicial interference would be justified only with evidence of the board's abuse of discretionary authority.

As in the preceding case reported, the court was not influenced by plaintiff's contention that "the requirement to maintain a 'uniform system of public schools, which shall be open to all children of the State . . .' must include the extracurricular activities and not merely the academic pursuits since the latter made up only a part of the total school program" (*Id.* at 720).

In response to the argument "that all students attending school should be accorded equal privileges and advantages," the court replied: "But the participation in extracurricular activities must necessarily be subject to regulations as to eligibility. Engaging in them is a privilege which may be claimed only in accordance with the standards set up for participation . . ." (*Id.* at 721).

(5) *Board of Directors of Independent School Dist. of Waterloo v. Green,* 259 Iowa 1260, 147 N.W.2d 854 (1961).

With this case there was evidence that the precedent established by *Kissick* was beginning to totter. Here the board of education adopted a policy barring married students from participation in extracurricular activities. A high school boy who was a regular player on the basketball team married just before his senior year. In accordance with the board policy he was denied the right to play on the team. The boy sought and obtained an injunction from the district court preventing enforcement of the rule. The board, in collaboration with the Iowa Association of School Boards, appealed to the Supreme Court which *reversed* the decision of the district court. In an attempt to defend its ruling, the Supreme Court stated:

> We conclude the rule adopted by defendant board barring married students from participating in extracurricular activities is neither arbitrary, unreasonable, irrational, unauthorized, nor unconstitutional. In taking this position we do not stand alone . . . (*Id.* at 860).

It is significant to note, however, that three of the justices dissented. In fact, the consensus was that this case marked the end of the judiciary's upholding school board rules and regulations designed to penalize married students by depriving them of the privilege to participate in *all* school activities. A rash of federal cases of the early 1970's bears out this contention.

(6) *Holt v. Shelton,* 341 F. Supp. 821 (M.D. Tenn. 1972).

This is the first case on the issue in which a *female* student was involved. She successfully sought an injunction prohibiting school officials from prohibiting her, because she was married, from participating in activities and functions other than those for which credit for graduation was given. The court's rationale in support of the girl is forcefully stated as follows:

> In the case at bar, the regulation which

plaintiff is challenging infringes upon her fundamental right to marry by severely limiting her right to an education. The defendants have failed utterly to show that the infringement upon either of these two rights promotes a "compelling" state interest. Indeed, they have failed to show that the regulation in question is even rationally related to — not to mention "necessary" to promote — *any* legitimate state interest at all. Instead it is apparent that the sole purpose and effect of the regulation is to discourage, by actually punishing, marriages which are perfectly legal under the laws of Tennessee and which are thus fully consonant with the public policy of the State. It is the opinion of the court that such a regulation is repugnant to the Constitution of the United States in that it impermissibly infringes upon the due process and equal protection of the law of those students who come within its ambit (*Id.* at 823).

(7) *Davis v. Meek,* 344 F. Supp. 298 (N.D. Ohio 1972). In this case a student was successful in a suit enjoining a school board from excluding him from participation in extracurricular activities because of his marriage. He was an honor student, an excellent baseball player and a good prospect for an athletic scholarship in several colleges.

The federal court admitted that in the past state courts have upheld board rules denying married students the right to participate in extracurricular activities — but sometimes with vigorous dissents. The federal courts have ruled against the board regulation mainly because of the constitutional right of marital privacy. For example, the court stated:

> . . . it seems clear that the effect of the enforcement of the rule which the defendants have promulgated under the color and authority of the state laws, is to put what may be an unendurable strain upon the plaintiff's marriage. . . . What greater invasion of marital privacy can there be than one which could totally destroy the marriage itself (*Id.* at 302).

(8) *Moran v. School Dist. #7, Yellowstone County,* 350 F. Supp. 1180 (D. Mont. 1972).

This case is quite similar to the one previously cited in which a preliminary injunction was granted to a married student who was held by the board to be ineligible to play varsity football. As has so often been charged by school officials that "presence of married students in extracurricular activities would result in reasonable likelihood of moral pollution." No factual evidence for this charge could be produced.

In its reliance on the present case:

> Montana Supreme Court has recognized the importance of extracurricular activities as an integral part of the total education process. Courts have begun to recognize that extracurricular activities such as football are "generally recognized as a fundamental ingredient of the educational process" (*Id.* at 1184).

Furthermore, the court stated:

> Since there is no authority expressly granted to the board to regulate marriages and since there is clear public policy with regard to marriage then to constitute a valid exercise of state law the school board's authority to discriminate on the basis of marriage must first be found in its expressed function of providing education and then balanced against the interest which it may violate (*Id.* at 1185).

(9) *Romans v. Crenshaw,* 354 F. Supp. 868 (S.D. Tex. 1972).

This is another case involving a *female* student. She was successful in a suit challenging a school regulation prohibiting "[A]ny student who is married or has been married, * * * from participating in any extracurricular activities."

The student plaintiff in this case had married at the age of fifteen and was divorced ten months later. During this time it was "undisputed that her performance in both conduct and curricular studies this semester has been exceptionally good" (*Id.* at 869).

The defendant school board presented the worn-out argument that "fraternization by married students is disruptive in the context of high school administration. It is argued that it will lead to undue interest in and discussion of sex by unmarried students." The court refuted this argument by stating: "In fact, the testimony reveals that sex education is taught in the 3rd, 4th and 5th grades in the elementary schools" (*Id.* at 869).

(10) *Hollon v. Mathis Independent School Dist.,* 358 F. Supp. 1269 (S.D. Tex. 1973).

In this case a temporary injunction was granted against enforcement of a school district policy prohibiting married students from engaging in interscholastic league athletic activities. The married student involved was a senior, seventeen years of age. He had been active in athletics, lettering in both football and basketball. He was considered to be a good athlete and was in line for a college scholarship, and intended to continue his education on the college level.

A school board policy in effect since 1959 disallowed married students to participate in interscholastic athletic contests. Even though the student was lawfully married, he was barred from participating in the athletic contests.

The school officials attempted to justify their policy by referring to the alarming number of marriages and drop-outs. The court's reaction is revealed in the following declaration:

> The Superintendent and the members of the School Board are certainly to be commended on a consistent effort to meet these most serious problems attendant with the high rate of high school drop-outs. However, the court has decided there is no justifiable relationship between the marriage of high school athletes and the overall drop-out problem; nor does it appear that preventing a good athlete, although married, from continuing to play in whatever game he may excell, would in any way deter other marriages or otherwise enhance the drop-out problem (*Id.* at 1271).

(11) *Bell v. Lone Oak Independent School Dist.,* 507 S.W.2d 636 (Tex. 1974).

That the state courts will fall in line with the federal courts is evidenced by the last court decision reported on the issue at the time of this writing. In the instant case a student was successful in having enjoined the enforcement of a school regulation designed to prohibit married students from participating in extracurricular activities.

The portion of the litigated regulation stipulated that:

> The married student cannot be elected to an office, or if already elected, must resign; . . . cannot participate in athletics, pep squad, class plays, social events such as junior-senior banquet, football banquet, etc.; . . . (*Id.* at 637).

Although the court was reluctant to deal with this much-litigated issue again, it did, and ruled decisively in favor of the student. In so doing, the court declared:

> The quoted rule of the Lone Oak Independent School District sets up a classification of individuals to be treated differently from the remainder of the school students without being designed to promote a compelling state interest. . . . Appellees have not shown a clear and present danger to the other students' physical and emotional safety and well-being, or any other danger to the students, faculty, or school property, nor any substantial or material danger to the operation of the public schools by allowing married students to participate in athletics. The burden of proof is upon the school district to show that its rule should be upheld as a necessary restraint to promote a compelling state interest.

It is the public policy of this state to encourage marriage rather than living together unmarried. To promote that public policy, we have sanctioned by statute the marriage ceremony . . . and through the years have jealously guarded the bonds of matrimony. It therefore seems illogical to say that a school district can make a rule punishing a student for entering into a status authorized and sanctioned by the laws of this state. We find no logical bases for such rule. We are not unmindful of the decision in *Kissick* . . . involving a situation very similar to the one in this case. There the court held that it was not arbitrary, capricious, discriminatory or unreasonable to bar married students from participating in athletics or other extracurricular activities. Our holding in this case is in direct opposition to *Kissick,* . . .

We have chosen not to follow the decision in *Kissick* . . . because we feel that the rule there should be abandoned for one that is non-discriminatory and which does not violate constitutionally guaranteed rights . . . (*Id.* at 638).

§ 6.5. Deprivation of privileges for members of secret societies.

School patrons and high school students have frequently questioned the authority of legislatures to enact antifraternity statutes, as well as that of school boards to impose restrictions and penalties on those who affiliate with the secret societies. As evidenced by the number of court cases, the controversy has been so severe as to often culminate in litigation. Statutes and school board regulations dealing with the issue have been tested in the courts of record of seventeen states in the past century. Since the issues and the judicial reactions have been quite similar in all the cases, only representative cases will be referred to here in detail.

(1) *Holroyd v. Eibling,* 174 Ohio St. 296, 188 N.E.2d 797 (1963).

In this case an Ohio court was petitioned for a permanent injunction to enjoin the school board of Columbus from enforcing a regulation which prohibited any student holding membership in a fraternity or sorority from participating in "... any athletic, literary, military, musical, dramatic, service, scientific, scholastic, and other similar activities of his school including honor societies, or honor organizations ..." (*Id.* at 799).

Plaintiff parents objected to the regulations on the grounds that if enforced, the school authorities would gain complete control of the students' activities and thus deny parents their responsibility to select associates for their children away from school and after school hours. The court, however, was not convinced by this argument and, accordingly, upheld the regulatory action of the school board. After reviewing and referring to a number of preceding court decisions on the issue, the Court of Appeals of Ohio stated:

... The rationale of these decisions is that

a board of education is vested with broad discretionary powers in adopting a policy prohibiting affiliation with such organizations in the government, management and discipline of the schools; that such regulations do not deprive the pupils or parents of any *natural* or constitutional rights or privileges; that, when, in the opinion of the school authorities, such organizations have a deleterious influence and are found to be inimical to the best interests of the school, a school board is authorized, even in the absence of a specific statute granting such power, to adopt regulations prohibiting them; and that such power is inherent in a board of education (*Id.* at 801).

Several other cases, marking the first, and perhaps the last, dealing with regulations designed to penalize high school student for affiliating with secret societies, are referred to briefly below.

(2) *Wayland v. Board of School Directors,* 43 Wash. 441, 86 P. 642 (1906).

This is the first case reported by a court of record. It developed from a board regulation denying fraternity members the right to participate in the extracurricular activities of the school such as athletics, literary clubs, and music organizations. The student involved challenged the regulation because the fraternity was not a school affair and therefore the board's action was illegal. Nevertheless, the Supreme Court of Washington upheld the school board.

(3) *Wilson v. Board of Educ. of Chicago,* 233 Ill. 464, 84 N.E. 697 (1908).

Two years later a similar case was adjudicated in

Illinois. Here a school board adopted a rule whereby students who were members of a secret society would be denied the privilege of representing the school "in any literary or athletic contest." Action was brought to enjoin the enforcement of the rule on the ground that it was unreasonable, a violation of the natural rights of students, and discriminatory. The Supreme Court of Illinois did not agree and ruled that the board "could control and manage the schools and adopt rules and regulations necessary for that purpose."

(4) *Wright v. Board of Educ. of St. Louis,* 245 Mo. 466, 246 S.W. 43 (1922).

A legal precedent was temporarily reversed in the ruling of the Supreme Court of Missouri. Here it was shown that a school board passed a regulation to prohibit fraternity members from representing the school in any capacity or from participating in graduation exercises. The court ruled that the board presented insufficient evidence to prove that the secret societies were a detriment to the efficient operation of the school. This was the first and only case in which an antifraternity rule was declared illegal by a court.

(5) *Antell v. Stokes,* 287 Mass. 103, 191 N.E. 407 (1934).

This case differed from most of the others in that expulsion was resorted to, instead of curtailment of participation in extracurricular activities for violation of an antifraternity rule. In upholding the action of the school committee, the court made the following terse statement: "The power to make rules would be vain without the capacity to annex reasonable penalties for their violation."

(6) *Coggins v. Board of Educ. of City of Durham,* 223 N.C. 763, 28 S.E.2d 527 (1944).

In this case pupils were required to sign pledge cards of nonaffiliation with secret societies. Those who refused to sign the pledge cards would be denied the right to participate in numerous extracurricular activities, the most effective one being intramural and interscholastic activities or contests. In the "test case" the Supreme Court of North Carolina decided in favor of the board — emphasizing that: "The right to attend school and claim the benefits afforded by the public school system is the right to attend subject to all lawful rules and regulations prescribed for the government thereof."

(7) *Wilson v. Abilene Independent School Dist.,* 190 S.W.2d 406 (Tex. Civ. App. 1945).

Despite the firmness of the North Carolina decision, similar litigation developed in Texas the very next year. Again the requirement to sign a pledge was challenged as being "discriminatory, unreasonable and illegal." A class suit brought to enjoin enforcement of the rule was refused by the court. Plaintiffs were advised that the rule was within the legal exercise of power delegated to local trustees by the legislature.

(8) *Burkitt v. School Dist. No. 1, Multnomah County,* 195 Ore. 471, 246 P.2d 566 (1952).

The lengthiest case on the fraternity issue was decided in Oregon in 1952. After a year of controversy over an early Oregon statute forbidding secret societies of any kind, a board resolution was adopted whereby pupils who joined such societies would be subject to suspension or expulsion. Plaintiffs argued that the rule violated the right of assemblage and was an invasion of parental authority since the clubs met outside of school hours. In disagreeing with this contention, the court followed the reasoning in previous decisions on the issue by calling attention to the fact that by enrolling in and attending the public schools, the pupils came under the control and discipline of school officials.

(9) *Passel v. Fort Worth Independent School Dist.,* 429 S.W.2d 917 (Tex. Civ. App. 1968).

Here parents unsuccessfully sought to prevent enforcement of a statute which prohibited secret societies in public schools. They contended that the statute "constitutes an invasion of the right of parental control over their children." In refuting this contention, the court stated: "We believe that our duly constituted independent school districts with appropriate guidance from the Legislature should run our public school system."

(10) *Robinson v. Sacramento City Unified School Dist.,* 245 Cal. App. 2d 278, 53 Cal. Rptr. 781 (1966).

Although there have been relatively fewer court cases involving sororities, the courts are no less emphatic in declaring their illegality. For example, a case arose in California in which a member of a girls' "secret society" unsuccessfully attempted to have invalidated a rule of the school board which "prohibited a fraternity, sorority, or club in which the membership was determined secretly." Even though admitting worthy objectives of the club, the court declared:

> High school fraternities, sororities and clubs undoubtedly accomplish good, mostly to those who belong to them, giving them a sense of security, a feeling of being wanted. But the school board has said the harm these societies do outweighs the good, that they are "inimical" to the "government, discipline and morale of the pupils" (*Id.* at 789).

Chapter 7

CONCLUSIONS AND IMPLICATIONS

§ 7.1. The in loco parentis theory.

This Latin phrase was meaningful during the period before *public* education and compulsory school attendance. As Blackstone described it, a parent delegated part of his parental authority over his child to the schoolmaster for purposes of restraint and correction during school hours. With the advent of compulsory school attendance, however, some parents challenged the assumed right of school authorities to govern the conduct and other rights of their children.

Consequently, the *in loco parentis* concept entered into many of the court cases concerning student discipline. As the theory expanded to include matters designed to protect the morals, welfare and safety of students and to determine their school attendance, appearance, and curricular activities without parental concurrence, the legality of its application became more questionable.

According to writers in the field of school law, the *in loco parentis* concept is no longer very meaningful. The tremendous changes in size and administration of school programs, plus the extension of the doctrine beyond its original stipulation "as may be necessary to answer the purpose for which he is employed," has reduced the viability of the doctrine. So its inclusion as a defense argument in student disciplinary cases has just about ended.

§ 7.2. Due process and student discipline.

The great majority of court cases concerning student disciplinary actions during the past decade have focused on the constitutional rights of due process. In virtually all student disciplinary cases the basic question is whether students may be "deprived of life, liberty, or property without due process of law" as provided in the Fifth Amendment, or in the Fourteenth Amendment, which extends these rights to "any person within its jurisdiction the equal protection of the laws."

Some student disciplinary cases involve *procedural due process* rights, whereas others involve *substantive due process* rights. Briefly stated, *procedural due process* rights mean that one cannot be deprived of a right before being given a notice of the charge against him and the necessary opportunity to defend himself. *Substantive due process* requires that laws will operate equally with protection from arbitrary action.

Over the past two decades there have been approximately as many student disciplinary cases involving procedural due process as cases involving substantive due process. As a result of the historical decision in the *Gault* case, procedural due process has come into sharper focus in recent years. Consequently, a majority of the cases referred to in Chapter 3 deal with procedural due process.

The scope of due process applicability perplexes school officials as to just how far they must go in granting young students all the formal steps of procedural due process, regardless of the gravity of the student's alleged misconduct. Most courts will honor the reasonable judgment of the school administrators.

§ 7.3. Administration of corporal punishment.

Corporal punishment of students is contemporaneous with the *in loco parentis* concept. Its purpose is to inflict physical pain as a deterrent for misbehavior. As a punitive measure, it is prohibited in two states, permissible or required in forty-eight states, and effective in virtually none.

Its decline over the past century has been due mainly to a change in the social viewpoint, its ineffectiveness in bringing about improved behavior — especially at the high school level — and the limited degree to which it can legally be imposed. The majority of court cases indicate that if corporal punishment is administered at all, it should: (1) be in conformance with statutory enactment; (2) be for the purpose of correction without malice; (3) not be cruel or excessive as to leave permanent injuries; and (4) be suited to the age and sex of the offender. With these restraints it is understandable that corporal punishment in the public schools is not very effective as a disciplinary practice.

Many writers on the issue claim that corporal punishment is not only ineffective but instead injurious to the child who is being punished and to the person who administers the punishment. Since it is based on a psychology of fear and humiliation, it may create antagonism between student and teachers, thereby complicating the punitive process.

The impropriety as well as the illegality of corporal punishment is well summed up by a justice of the United States Supreme Court who stated that: "Corporal punishment offends contemporary concepts of decency and human dignity and precepts of civilization which we profess to possess. The broad characterization of corporal punishment as offensive to contemporary values cannot be ignored."

§ 7.4. Exclusionary practices: suspension — expulsion.

The legal principle is firmly established that school authorities may *suspend* or *expel* students who disobey reasonable board rules or regulations. With the escalating violence, vandalism and misbehavior in the public schools today, and the diminution of corporal punishment as a means of abating the misbehavior, school authorities often exercise their discretionary prerogative to employ the alternatives of suspension and expulsion.

It is generally assumed that "suspension" constitutes an act of a professional member of the staff and is for a short period of time; whereas "expulsion" is an act of the school board and is for a relatively long period of time — sometimes permanent.

Legislatures, school officials and the judiciary have often been uncertain as to what constitutes a "short term" suspension as contrasted with a "long term" suspension — the latter of which would necessitate the more formal processes of due process. In 1975, the United States Supreme Court attempted to bring the issue to rest by ruling in *Goss v. Lopez* that students suspended for *short periods* of time were nevertheless entitled to minimal due process under the Fourteenth Amendment. The ruling struck down an Ohio law which authorized school officials to suspend a student for ten days or less without going through the formal due-process procedures required for long-term suspension or expulsion.

Whether the decision in this case is the final word is doubtful in the minds of many. After all, it was a split (5-4) decision with Justices White, Douglas, Brennan, and Stewart representing the majority, while Chief Justice Burger and Justices Blackmun and Rehnquist (all appointees of former President Nixon) supported the dissenting opinion.

The other United States Supreme Court decision in 1975 (*Wood v. Strickland*) dealing with suspensions, involved an additional issue, namely, the liability of school officials for acts which deprive students of rights, privileges, and immunities guaranteed by the Constitution. Although the court did rule that "absolute immunity" would not be justified for school officials whose actions subject students to intentional and inexcusable deprivations, many analysts have pushed the "panic button" prematurely. Even the dissenting justices suggest that the court's decision will cause citizens to refrain from serving on boards of education for fear of monetary liability. A careful reading of the majority opinion, however, should give assurance that school board members who act honestly and in good faith will be free from personal liability.

§ 7.5. Unorthodox practices of disciplining.

When organizing school-law issues and court cases into chapters, there is usually some difficulty in categorizing those miscellaneous cases which vary from the norm. This chapter, therefore, deals with cases pertaining to disciplinary practices which differ from the more familiar practices of corporal punishment, suspension and expulsion.

To many persons these cases may not seem to be extremely significant. Since, they refer to deprivation of school privileges, they are, however, significant to those who suffer the deprivation to the extent of motivating litigation.

In most instances the administrative acts which deprive some students of privileges afforded others are poorly conceived, unnecessary, unreasonable and illegal. School administrators who do not know this are lacking in good administrative judgment and a knowledge of school law.

SELECTED BIBLIOGRAPHY

Albert, John J. "Due Process in Secondary Schools." *Marquette Law Review,* Vol. 54 (1971), pp. 358-69.

"A Legal Memorandum: Student Discipline: Suspension and Expulsion." *National Association of Secondary School Principals.* Reston, Va. 22091 (June 1975).

American Jurisprudence, *Constitutional Law,* Vol. 16 (1964), pp. 941-47.

Anson, Ronald J. "The Educator's Response to Goss and Wood." *Phi Delta Kappan* (September, 1975), pp. 16-19.

Aron, Peter S. and Martin L. Katz. "Corporal Punishment in the Public Schools." *Harvard Civil Rights: Civil Liberties Law Review,* Vol. 6 (1971), pp. 583-94.

Bayh, Birch. "Opening Statement at Hearings on School Violence and Vandalism: Nature and Extent." (June 17, 1975).

Blackstone. *Commentaries of the Laws of England,* 453 (T. Cooley, ed., 1884).

Bowdoin, W. Roderick. "Balancing in Loco Parentis and the Constitution," *University of Florida Law Review,* Vol. 26 (1974), pp. 271-88.

Buss, William G. "Procedural Due Process for School Discipline," *University of Pennsylvania Law Review,* Vol. 119 (1971), pp. 545-641.

"Discipline and Student Rights." *Center for Law and Education.* Harvard University (July 1975).

"Gault: What Now For The Juvenile Court?" *Institute of Continuing Legal Education,* Ann Arbor, Michigan (1968).

Gunn, Thomas A. "In Loco Parentis and Due Process," *Baylor Law Review,* Vol. 26 (1974), pp. 678-86.

Hudgins, H. C., Jr. "School Administrators and the Courts: A Review of Recent Decisions," *Educational Research Service, Inc.* (1975).

_____. "The Discipline of Secondary School Students and Procedural Due Process," *Wake Forest Law Review,* Vol. 7 (1970), pp. 32-48.

Ladd, Edward T. "Allegedly Disruptive Student Behavior and the

Legal Authority of School Officials," *Journal of Public Law,* Vol. 19 (1970), pp. 219-20.

Lillie, John C. "Restrictions on the Infliction of Corporal Punishment: Spoiling the Rod," *North Carolina Law Review,* Vol. 50 (1972), pp. 911-17.

Massachusetts Gen. Laws Ann. Ch. 71-37 G. Supp. (1973), p. 30.

Mawdsley, Ralph D. "In Loco Parentis: A Balancing of Interests," *Illinois Bar Journal,* Vol. 61 (August 1973), pp. 638-46.

McCarthy, Mary Dianne. "Humanitarianism and Corporal Punishment," *Education,* Vol. 95, No. 3 (Spring 1975), pp. 212-215.

New Jersey Stat. Ann. 18A:6-1 (1968), p. 77.

Report of the Children's Defense Fund of the Washington Research Project, Inc. "Children Out of School in America." (1974).

Report of the Subcommittee to Investigate Juvenile Delinquency. "Our Nation's Schools — A Report Card: 'A' in School Violence and Vandalism," U.S. Government Printing Office, Washington, D.C. (1975).

Report of the Task Force of the NEA. "Model Law Outlining Corporal Punishment." The Report (1972), p. 29-a.

Seaton, Hal W. and Regis Q. McKnight. "Lack of Authority: A Crisis in Education," *American Secondary Education,* (March 1975), pp. 6-7.

Smith, Donald E. "Surviving Student Behavior Problems," *American Secondary Education,* (June 1975), p. 29.

Vernon, Thomas Edward. "Legality and Propriety of Disciplinary Practices in the Public Schools," unpublished Ed. D. Dissertation, Department of Education, Duke University (1968).

Volz, Marlin M. "The Principal in the Role of Loco Parentis," *Law and the School Principal.* The W. H. Anderson Company, Cincinnati (1961), pp. 123-33.

Youngblood, William L. "Recent Decisions," *Mississippi Law Journal,* Vol. 44 (1973), pp. 550-55.

TABLE OF CASES

Dorsey v. Bale, 521 S.W.2d 76 (Ky. Ct. of App. 1975), § 6.2.

Duda v. Gaines, 12 N.J. Super. 326, 79 A.2d 695 (1951), § 2.3.

Ector County Independent School Dist. v. Hopkins, 518 S.W.2d 576 (Tex. Civ. App. 1975), § 5.4.

Edwards v. Jersey Shore Area School Dist., 7 Pa. Cmwlth. 636, 301 A.2d 116 (1973), § 5.4.

Farrell v. Joel, 437 F.2d 160 (2d Cir. 1971), § 3.4.

Fortman v. Texarkana School Dist. No. 7, 514 S.W.2d 720 (Ark. 1974), § 5.4.

Gault, In re, 387 U.S. 1 (1967), § 3.2.

Glaser v. Marietta, 351 F. Supp. 555 (W.D. Pa. 1972), § 4.3.

Goetz v. Ansell, 477 F.2d 636 (2d Cir. 1973), § 5.5.

Gonyaw v. Gray, 361 F. Supp. 366 (D.Vt. 1973), § 4.3.

Gonzalez v. School Dist. of Phil., 8 Pa. Cmwlth. 130, 301 A.2d 99 (1973), § 5.4.

Gordon v. Oak Park School Dist. No. 97, 24 Ill. App. 3d 131, 320 N.E.2d 389 (1974), §§ 4.3, 6.3.

Goss v. Lopez, 95 S. Ct. 729 (Ohio 1975), § 5.6.

Graber v. Kniola, 52 Mich. App. 269, 216 N.W.2d 925 (1974), § 5.5.

Graham v. Knutzen, 351 F. Supp. 642 (D. Neb. 1972), § 5.5.

Greene v. Moore, 373 F. Supp. 1194 (N.D. Tex. 1974), § 5.4.

Guerrieri v. Tyson, 147 Pa. Super. 239, 24 A.2d 468 (1942), § 2.3.

H., In re, 78 Misc. 2d 412, 357 N.Y.S.2d 384 (Fam. Ct. 1974), § 2.5.

Hannah v. Larche, 363 U.S. 420 (1960), § 3.1.

Heritage v. Dodge, 64 N.H. 297, 9 A. 722 (1887), § 4.2.

Hollon v. Mathis Independent School Dist., 358 F. Supp. 1269 (S.D. Tex. 1973), § 6.4.

Holroyd v. Eibling, 174 Ohio St. 296, 188 N.E.2d 797 (1963), § 6.5.

Holt v. Shelton, 341 F. Supp. 821 (M.D. Tenn. 1972), § 6.4.

Houston v. Prosser, 361 F. Supp. 295 (N.D. Ga. 1973), § 5.5.

Indiana State Personnel Bd. v. Jackson, 224 Ind. 321, 192 N.E.2d 740 (1963), § 4.2.

Ingraham v. Wright, 498 F.2d 248 (5th Cir. 1974), § 4.3.

Johnson v. Horace Mann Mut. Ins. Co., 241 So. 2d 588 (La. 1970), § 4.3.

"K.C." v. Board of Educ. of Collingwood (Decision of the N.J. Comm'r of Educ., June 20, 1973), § 6.1.

People v. Ball, 58 Ill. 2d 36, 317 N.E.2d 54 (1974), § 4.3.
People v. De Caro, 17 Ill. App. 3d 553, 308 N.E.2d 196 (1974), § 4.3.
People v. Ekerold, 211 N.Y. 386, 105 N.E. 670 (1914), § 2.5.
People in Interest of K. P., 514 P.2d 1131 (Colo. 1973), § 5.4.
Perry v. Grenada Municipal Separate School Dist., 300 F. Supp. 748 (N.D. Miss. 1969), § 5.5.
Pierce v. Society of Sisters of Holy Names, Etc., 268 U.S. 510, 45 S. Ct. 571 (1925), § 2.4.
Pound v. Holladay, 322 F. Supp. 1000 (Miss. 1971), § 2.6.
Pugsley v. Sellmeyer, 158 Ark. 247, 250 S.W. 538 (1923), § 5.3.
R.H., a minor, by his parent and guardian, ad litem v. Board of Educ. of Township of Delano (Decision by the N.J. Comm'r of Educ., Decision 1974), § 6.1.
"R. K." v. Board of Educ. of Township of Lakewood (Decision of the Comm'r of Educ., June 19, 1973), § 5.8.
Robinson v. Sacramento City Unified School Dist., 245 Cal. App. 2d 278, 53 Cal. Rptr. 781 (1966), § 6.5.
Romans v. Crenshaw, 354 F. Supp. 868 (S.D. Tex. 1972), § 6.4.
Roy v. Continental Ins. Co., 313 So. 2d 349 (La. App. 1975), § 4.3.
Sapp v. Renfroe, 372 F. Supp. 1193 (N.D. Ga. 1974), § 5.4.
Simms v. School Dist. No. 1, Multnomah County, 508 P.2d 236 (Ore. App. 1973), § 4.3.
Sims v. Board of Educ. of Independent School Dist. No. 22, 329 F. Supp. 678 (N.M. 1971), §§ 3.4, 4.3, 4.4.
Smith v. Miller, 514 P.2d 377 (Kan. 1973), § 5.5.
St. Ann v. Palisi, 495 F.2d 423 (5th Cir. 1974), § 5.5.
Starkey v. Board of Educ. of Davis County School Dist., 14 Utah 2d 227, 381 P.2d 718 (1963), § 6.4.
State v. Bailey, 157 Ind. 324, 61 N.E. 730 (1901), § 2.4.
State ex rel. Sherman v. Hyman, 180 Tenn. 99, 171 S.W. 2d 822 (1942), § 3.3.
State v. Massa, 95 N.J. Super. 382, 231 A.2d 252 (1967), § 2.4.
State v. Pendergrass, 19 N.C. 365, 31 Am. Dec. 416 (1837), § 4.2.
State v. Stevenson, 27 Ohio App. 2d 223, 189 N.E.2d 181 (1962), § 6.4.

Index

A

ALCOHOLIC BEVERAGES.
Suspension and expulsion.
Intoxication as grounds for suspension or expulsion, §5.4.

APPEARANCE.
Regulation of pupil appearance, §2.6.
Suspension.
Recent cases invalidating suspension for personal
appearance, §5.5.

ASSOCIATIONS.
Secret societies.
Deprivation of privileges for members of secret societies,
§6.5.

ATTENDANCE.
Compulsory school attendance.
Right to counsel.
Effect of In re Gault, §3.3.

B

BLAME FOR STUDENT MISCONDUCT, §1.1.

C

CLOTHING.
Regulation of student appearance, §2.6.

COMPULSORY ATTENDANCE.
Suspension and expulsion.
Absenteeism as grounds for suspension or expulsion, §5.4.

UNORTHODOX PRACTICES OF DISCIPLINING—Cont'd
Summary and conclusion as to unorthodox practices of
disciplining, §7.5.

UNWED MOTHERS.
Pregnancy as grounds for suspension.
Decisions invalidating suspension, §5.5.

W

WHIPPING.
Corporal punishment.
See CORPORAL PUNISHMENT.

WITNESSES.
Right of confrontation and cross-examination of witnesses.
Effect of In re Gault, §3.3.

Jl